United

The Staggering Message of the Kingdom

JEFF WICKHAM

COME AND FEAST
HERNANDO, MISSISSIPPI

Cover illustration and design by Shane Fredericks and Justin Oeftger

Proofing by Daun Redfield

Interior design by Ken McFarland

Back cover portrait by Mark Istvanko

United: The Staggering Message of the Kingdom

Unless otherwise marked, Scripture quotations are taken from the New American Standard Bible®, copyright © 1960, 1962, 1963, 1968, 1971, 1972, 1973, 1975, 1977, 1995 by The Lockman Foundation. Used by permission (www.Lockman.org).

Scripture quotations marked NKJV are taken from the New King James Version®. Copyright © 1982 by Thomas Nelson. Used by permission. All rights reserved.

Scripture quotations marked NIV are taken from the Holy Bible, New International Version®, NIV®. Copyright © 1973, 1978, 1984, 2011 by Biblica, Inc.™ Used by permission of Zondervan. All rights reserved worldwide.

Scripture quotations marked KJV are taken from the Holy Bible, King James Version.

Scripture quotations marked ASV are taken from the Holy Bible, American Standard Version.

Some names and identifying details in stories have been changed in order to protect the identity of those involved.

ISBN: 978-0-9972516-0-9

Publisher's Cataloging-in-Publication Data

Names: Wickham, Jeff.

Title: United : the staggering message of the kingdom / Jeff Wickham.

Description: Hernando, MS : Come and Feast, 2016.

Identifiers: ISBN 978-0-9972516-0-9 (pbk.) | ISBN 978-0-9972516-1-6 (ebook: Kindle) | ISBN 978-0-9972516-2-3 (ebook: EPUB)

Subjects: LCSH: Spiritual life—Christianity. | God (Christianity)--Simplicity. | Salvation--Christianity. | Kingdom of God. | BISAC: RELIGION / Christian Life / Spiritual Growth. | RELIGION / Christian Theology / Soteriology.

Classification: LCC BV4501.3 .W52 2016 (print) | LCC BV4501.3 (ebook) | DDC: 248.4--dc23.

For speaking and conference information e-mail or call:

Jeff Wickham

Come and Feast

(662) 469-5899

info@comeandfeast.org

www.comeandfeast.org

Acknowledgements

It is with profound gratitude that I would like to thank the following people for their contributions to this book:

Amy Wickham—Your love is a taste of heaven. It is a deep joy to be married to you, my dearest earthly friend, my confidant, and my soul mate. Being teamed up with you enables me to do far more than I could without you. Regarding this book specifically, thank you for all of your inputs, edits, and critiques. They were invaluable for distilling these ideas into polished form. Thank you for your patience with the thousands of hours spent on this project, your understanding of the great burden to share this message, and for carrying a disproportionate amount of home responsibilities during this time. It seems my ability to compensate you pales in comparison to the sacrifices you have made. It is my prayer that God will look upon your devotion to Him and to me, and repay you far beyond the limits of human rewards.

Gordon Kainer, Dan Martella, Daniel Privat, and Steve Wickham—Thank you for reviewing the first draft of this book. Your encouragement, criticisms, and suggestions dramatically improved the final product.

Floyd Bresee—Thank you for teaching me the fundamentals of preaching. The format you suggested for biblical and interesting speaking formed the foundation of the sermons that ultimately became this book. Virtually every page has been influenced by your advice.

Tim Lale—Thank you for the meticulous editing, the guidance regarding the publishing process, and your suggestions for additional resources. Your contributions took this book to an entirely new level.

Contents

Part 1

The Message of Unity

CHAPTER ONE

The All-Important Attitude

On the morning of December 22, 1991, twenty-two-year-old James Scott stepped out of the trekking lodge at Phedi in the Nepalese Himalayas. He and a trekking partner intended to hike over the Laurebinayak Pass to Kathmandu. A snowstorm descended upon them, and when they could not agree on whether to proceed or turn back, they amicably parted ways. James set out on a course that he thought would lead back to civilization, but the snow obscured the trail, and he lost his way. He eventually went miles off course and became hopelessly lost in the rugged landscape and deepening snow. Three days later, he took shelter under a rock overhang, hoping that either he would be spotted by a helicopter or that the snow would thaw enough that he could make progress.

For the next ten days he was extremely hungry. He had eaten all of his provisions in the first two days, and food became his preoccupation. At first he craved junk food, then home cooking, and then fresh fruit. He began to sample all vegetation within sight. Some bamboo growing nearby was fibrous and left a gritty feeling in his mouth. Pine needles from the nearby trees were bitter. Another plant had leaves that tasted horribly inedible. He tried a small plant that had

9

a spicy taste, but it provided him no substantial calories. He found a caterpillar and ate it but never found any more. Day by day he grew gaunter as the effects of starvation grew.

In the meantime, his family launched a relentless search effort, with people searching by foot and a helicopter searching by air. Day after day they combed the mountains, hoping against hope that they might still find James alive. Finally, forty-two days after his disappearance, when he was weak and near death, the rescue helicopter spotted him. A rescue party reached him on foot later that day, and the helicopter returned at first light the following day and airlifted him to safety.[1]

Just as James tried everything available that might satisfy his hunger, we in our own lives try many things to satisfy the hunger in our hearts. A career, entertainment, relationships, and a thousand other things seem to promise fulfillment, but after their temporary pleasure ceases, we find that a nameless craving remains. One thing, and only one thing, fills this yearning. The food and drink that truly satisfy the soul's craving are the words of Jesus internalized in one's life.

Jesus gave two great signs that were designed to draw attention to the true food and drink. For the first sign, He changed water into wine, and for the second, He changed one boy's lunch into a feast that fed a multitude. In this chapter we will closely inspect these two signs to see what Jesus meant by them.

Just three days after calling His first disciples, Jesus attended a wedding feast in Cana. His mother must have been

---

1. Mark D. Zimmerman, Kana Appadurai, James G. Scott, Leon B. Jellett, and Frank H. Garlick, "Case History," *Survival* 127, no. 5 (Sept. 1, 1997), 405–409, http://questgarden.com/50/64/9 /070904095633/files/James_Eats_Snow_Article.doc; Eric Bailey, "James Scott: How I Survived," *The Sun Herald*, Mar. 8, 1992, http://www.medicaltranslation.com.au/medical-translation -articles/1992/3/8/james-scott-how-i-survived/.

helping with the festivities, because part way through the feast she came to Jesus with an indirect request, saying, "They have no more wine." Such a lack was an embarrassing breach of hospitality. Once, my wife and I invited some people over for dinner, but somehow I misjudged the amount of food relative to the number of guests. We sat down to eat, and as the first people cleaned their plates and began getting seconds, the food ran out. All that remained were a couple of slices of bread politely left on the cutting board. Unfortunately, on that particular day we had no other food that could quickly be prepared and added to the meal. It was a breach of hospitality for which I was mortified, and that was only with about ten people at a common dinner. You can imagine how the bride and groom would feel at their wedding in Cana when, on one of the most special occasions in their lives, it became apparent that they had failed to adequately prepare for their guests. They had tried to prepare, but their provisions came short of the goal, and their friends and guests were left unsatisfied. In this context Jesus drew attention to what truly satisfies.

Jesus' Blood Is True Drink

Mary knew her son's character well, for she had lived with Him for thirty years. She knew that it would take only a suggestion of the need, and Jesus would do all within His power to supply the lack. However, He responded in a rather strange way. He replied, " 'Woman, what does that have to do with us? My hour has not yet come' " (John 2:4). What did He mean, "My hour has not yet come"? His hour for what? For doing miracles? His mother was not asking Him to do a miracle, only to help them with the provisions. And if the time was not right for a miracle, He would not have performed one that day.

Every other time in the book of John that Jesus referred to His "time" or His "hour," He was talking about His death.

When the Feast of Tabernacles was approaching, Jesus' brothers tried to encourage Him to go to Judea and act publically so He could show Himself to the world, but Jesus said, "My time is not yet here." Jesus' time eventually did come, and He went up to a feast in a very public way, as His brothers had suggested years before. He rode a donkey through the gates of Jerusalem, with thousands thronging around Him. Less than a week later, He was dead.

One time Jesus was teaching in the temple. The leaders wanted to seize Him, but "no man laid his hand on Him, because His hour had not yet come" (John 7:30). A few days later, Jesus was again teaching in the temple, and the crowd was enraged by His claims, but still "no one seized Him, because His hour had not yet come" (John 8:20).

About three days before He was crucified, Jesus was in the temple, and some Greeks sought Him out. He said to them,

> "The hour has come for the Son of Man to be glorified. Truly, truly, I say to you, unless a grain of wheat falls into the earth and dies, it remains alone; but if it dies, it bears much fruit. He who loves his life loses it, and he who hates his life in this world will keep it to life eternal. . . . Now My soul has become troubled; and what shall I say, 'Father, save Me from this hour'? But for this purpose I came to this hour" (John 12:23–25, 27).

The hour to which Jesus often referred was the time when He would give His blood that would quench the thirst of the world.

When Jesus' mother told Him at the wedding, "They have no more wine," and He provided all that they needed, Jesus was pointing them to the true drink He would later give that would indeed satisfy the thirst of their hearts. He gave them physical wine as a symbol of His blood that He would later provide.

The True Drink of Jesus' Blood Was Made by Crushing His Body

For a time my wife and I lived in California's wine country. Our house was in Alexander Valley, and two miles to the west was Dry Creek Valley. From our home we could see the hills that formed the northern terminus of the Napa Valley. The whole region was covered with thousands of acres of vineyards. During the fall, when the grapes ripened, workers would place the grapes in a special press that looked something like a large propane tank. On the inside of the press was an air bladder that, when filled with air, would expand and crush the grapes against the outside of the tank, squeezing out the grape juice. All that remained were the crushed and mutilated skins, seeds, and stems.

Grape juice is made by crushing the grapes; in like manner Jesus' body was crushed. He was killed and His blood shed so that a way could be made for us to partake of His blood. Isaiah prophesied, "He was pierced through for our transgressions, He was crushed for our iniquities; the chastening for our well-being fell upon Him, and by His scourging we are healed" (Isaiah 53:5). His piercing, His punishment, His crushing was what made a way for us to be healed. It is what provided His blood for us.

Jesus' Blood Provides Internal Cleansing

At the wedding, six stone water pots were sitting nearby that were normally used in the Jewish custom of purification. In the Jewish system of laws, a person could become ceremonially unclean in many ways. It could happen because they got sick, or because they touched a dead body, or because they touched the carcass of an unclean animal, or for a host of other reasons. They then had to go through a process of ceremonial purification, including washing their bodies with water. The water pots were used for this cleansing process. Jesus told the servants to fill the pots to the brim with water.

It is fitting that Jesus changed the water to wine in these water pots used for ceremonial purification. The water cleansed people on the outside, but Jesus' blood is what can truly cleanse us within. John wrote, "If we walk in the light as He Himself is in the light, we have fellowship with one another, and the blood of Jesus His Son cleanses us from all sin" (1 John 1:7).

My profession as an engineer is focused on designing medical devices. One time I was working on a surgical wound closure device, and our team needed to determine which color scheme provided the best visibility. The device had simple instructions on the outside, but since it was to be used in a surgical environment, it was likely to get blood on it during the procedure. In order to test several color schemes, one of our team members went down to a slaughter house south of town and brought back a five-gallon bucket of cow's blood. We spread the blood on the devices and determined which color scheme had the best visibility for the instructions.

When I told my oldest son about the experience, he replied, "Ugh! That is nasty!" Indeed it was disgusting. The point is, blood is not a cleansing agent; it is a life-giving agent. The Israelites were strictly forbidden to eat blood because " ' "the life of the flesh is in the blood, and I [God] have given it to you on the altar to make atonement for your souls" ' " (Leviticus 17:11). God gave this strict command, yet at the Last Supper, Jesus took a cup, gave thanks, and gave it to the disciples, and they all drank from it. He said to them, " 'This is My blood of the covenant, which is poured out for many' " (Mark 14:24). He gave them the blood of the grape as a symbol of His own blood. In the same way that they drank the juice, they were also to internalize His blood. The way Jesus' blood cleanses us is by giving us His life.

Faith Results in a Change

The servants followed Jesus' instructions to fill the water pots and then reported to Him that they had done as He had commanded. Then He told them to draw some out and take it to the head waiter. Now imagine for a moment that you are waiting tables in a restaurant. One of your customers selects a dish of lasagna from the menu, and you relay the message to the chef. Soon the chef tells you, "Your customer's order is ready," and then slides a peanut-butter-and-jelly sandwich across the counter to you. Would you not feel awkward about serving it to your customer, knowing they expect lasagna?

The servants at the wedding feast faced a similar dilemma. The head waiter was no doubt feeling stressed about the wine shortage. People were asking for more wine, and he was supposed to relay the embarrassing message, "There is no more wine." Such a stressful situation is not the time for a joke. How would he respond if the servants brought him water when he was expecting wine? Would they not fall out of his good graces? Nevertheless they acted on Jesus' instructions, even though it seemed to make no human sense. In other words, they exercised faith. Then, somewhere between when they dipped the utensil into the water pot and when the cup touched the head waiter's lips, the water was changed into wine.

In the same way, Jesus' instructions are often counterintuitive to our human understanding. Following His instructions sometimes seems as though it will lead to embarrassment or harm to ourselves, and yet if we act on them anyway, we find that in the process His words are changed into His Spirit.

Jesus' Words Are Delightful

When I was in high school I played in a steel drum band. We were taught to keep a pleasant expression on our faces while we performed. We dressed up in our colorful uniforms, smiled as we had been taught, and played our parts in the catchy tunes. The audiences smiled in return and let themselves be carried along by the music, then showered us with adulation and smiles. But for us it was just an outward show. The smiles were just a veneer that we put on for a time, and they belied the hidden turmoil so common in adolescent years. Had those in the audience been able to shadow us for a day and see the reality of our lives, they might have paused before showering us with praise.

The attraction of the world is like a show. The things of the world are like a shiny foil wrapper on a moldy crust of bread. It looks good on the outside, but it is disappointing when actually experienced. However, those who taste the words of Jesus are amazed at the quality. They will wonder why they had not tasted them sooner.

When the head waiter at the wedding touched the cup to his lips, he was amazed by the quality of the wine. He did not realize where it had come from, so he went to the groom and exclaimed, " 'Every man serves the good wine first, and when the people have drunk freely, then he serves the poorer wine; but you have kept the good wine until now' " (John 2:10).

When I first came to know Christ, I remember walking by the pansies in our front-yard flower bed. Many times before, I had walked by such scenes with hardly a notice, but now I was stopped by the lovely beauty. I mused to myself how God had created such things for us as a token of His love, and how He cares to fill our lives with happiness and joy. I went on that day with my heart overflowing with thankfulness to God for His goodness. Those flowers and many other things became a hundred times more meaningful to me because of my new-found relationship with God.

Jesus said, " 'Truly I say to you, there is no one who has left house or wife or brothers or parents or children, for the sake of the kingdom of God, who will not receive many times as much at this time and in the age to come, eternal life' " (Luke 18:29, 30). He was not saying that we will literally have many wives or parents or children but that what we have will become many times more meaningful.

Jesus' Blood Provides Life

There at the wedding in Cana, the physical drink that Jesus provided would help to sustain the physical lives of all who drank it. It provided energy and sustenance to their bodies. In like manner, Jesus' blood provides spiritual life for all who will drink it. Jesus prayed, " 'This is eternal life, that they may know You, the only true God, and Jesus Christ whom You have sent' " (John 17:3). Jesus is the one who provides life, and He does so by giving us His blood so that we may truly know Him.

So let's put all of the symbols and reality together, summarized in a table.

Symbol	Reality
Physical wine	Jesus' blood, which is true drink
Crushed grapes	Crushed body
Ceremonial washing	Internal cleansing
Faith—water to wine	Faith—teachings to Spirit
Head waiter's delight	Believer's joy
Physical life	Spiritual life

First, the wine represents the blood. As Jesus said, " 'Drink from it, all of you; for this is My blood of the covenant' " (Matthew 26:27, 28). Second, the blood is a symbol of the Spirit. "The life [the spirit] is in the blood." Third, the Spirit is embodied in Jesus' teachings. He told the disciples, " 'The words that I have spoken to you are spirit and are life' " (John 6:63).

You might remember the principle of equivalence from high school math, which states that if A = B and B = C, then A = C. Let's set up an equation based on the things we have learned here:

Wine = Blood = Spirit = Teachings

If you shorten that equation it becomes:

Wine = Teachings

Therefore, when Jesus changed the water to wine, He was trying to convey that His teachings truly satisfy the thirst of the heart. When we adopt the all-important attitude—when we wholeheartedly take in and act on Jesus' teachings, depending on Him for strength—His words soothe the craving of our hearts.

Life from One Man's Gift

Jesus later reiterated the lesson when He changed one boy's lunch into a feast that fed a whole multitude. A large crowd had gathered to listen as Jesus taught. Jesus said to Philip, " 'Where are we to buy bread, so that these may eat?' " (John 6:5).

Philip responded, " 'Two hundred denarii worth of bread is not sufficient for them, for everyone to receive a little' " (verse 7).

Andrew said to Jesus, " 'There is a lad here who has five barley loaves and two fish, but what are these for so many people?' " (verse 9). Perhaps he thought Jesus could at least share the lunch with one or two who were in particular need. In any case, that was enough for Jesus to do what he was going to do. So let's start unpacking the symbols. One boy sacrificed his lunch. His sacrifice led to more than five thousand people receiving physical sustenance. In the reality to which this symbol pointed, one man, Jesus, sacrificed His body. His sacrifice resulted in millions being given spiritual life.

Jesus Was Blessed

After Andrew brought the boy to Him, Jesus directed the disciples to have the people sit down. He then took that lunch, and the first thing He did was to bless it. He did not bless it because it needed to be fixed. There was nothing wrong with the food. He blessed it because He was showing the people a symbol. The substance to which this symbol pointed was that Jesus was blessed. The Father sanctified Jesus and sent Him into the world (John 10:36). To sanctify something means to set it apart for a holy use. Jesus was set apart by the Father for a holy use—He was blessed by the Father.

Jesus Was Broken

Jesus then took the food and broke it. Imagine again that you are waiting tables, and your customer orders the plate of lasagna. This time the chef prepares the right dish. You carry it to the customer, but before you slide it across the table to him, you pull out a knife and cut it into small pieces. Would your customer be surprised? He would probably leave you a very small tip. However, that is exactly what Jesus did with the bread and fish—He broke them into pieces.

In like manner Jesus' body was broken. John wrote, "In the beginning was the Word, and the Word was with God, and the Word was God. . . . And the Word became flesh, and dwelt among us" (John 1:1, 14). *The Word* is another name for Jesus. This name indicates that Jesus is embodied in a set of teachings. These teachings are beyond ordinary—they are alive because they contain His Spirit. By Jesus' body being broken, or by His death, Jesus made a way that we can eat His body. We can eat the Word. When we eat the Word, we internalize His Spirit. If we internalize His Spirit, then He considers us as part of Himself.

Jeremiah prophesied of this beautiful reality, saying, "Thy

words were found, and I did eat them; and thy word was unto me the joy and rejoicing of mine heart: for I am called by thy name, O LORD God of hosts" (Jeremiah 15:16, KJV). If we eat Jesus' body in the form of His teachings, we will be called by God's name.

Jesus' Teaching Was Given to the Disciples and Then to the World

Once Jesus broke the food, He gave it to His disciples, and they in turn gave it to the multitude. In like manner Jesus committed His teachings primarily to His disciples. They in turn were commissioned to share His words with the whole world.

Wakulla Springs in the panhandle of Florida is one of the largest springs in the world, with an average daily flow of 260 million gallons of water. The water flows from the Floridan Aquifer through several vents and then down the Wakulla River into the ocean. In a similar way, Jesus sent His teachings out through a small number of people, who then took it to the world.

Gather Up the Fragments

Finally Jesus told the disciples to gather the fragments of food, and they collected twelve baskets of leftovers. Here is a question: How many meals did each person in the multitude receive that day? One? Yet when the disciples gathered up the fragments, they had enough food left over for many meals, far more than they could eat before it spoiled. Just as the disciples gathered up the fragments and they had an abundance, so those who gather up the fragments of Jesus' teaching will have an abundance.

God has a way of making His will known, even though He very rarely uses audible words. We may not know much of God's will, but, speaking for myself, there has never been a time that I did not know of something that needed to be improved in me in order to come closer to God's will. Certainly, at times I have not been aware of anything significant that God wanted changed, but even in those times there were smaller things that I knew needed tweaking. If we gather up the fragments of Jesus' teaching, we will have plenty of food.

Summarizing the symbols and realities from this sign, we have:

Symbol	Reality
One boy gave and 5,000+ received physical sustenance	One man gave and millions received spiritual life
Food blessed	Jesus blessed
Food broken	Jesus' body broken
Food: Jesus to disciples to multitude	Teaching: Jesus to disciples to multitude
Fragments of food—twelve basketsful	Fragments of teaching—abundance

From what we see in these parallels, it is evident that Jesus was trying to teach the multitude that applying His teachings in one's life will satisfy the hunger of the heart.

That evening, Jesus crossed over to the other side of the lake without the crowds knowing it. The next day the people finally found Him and tried to strike up a conversation with Him, saying, " 'Rabbi, when did You get here?' " (John 6:25). Jesus brushed aside the formalities and immediately began explaining what He had done the day before. He said to them, " 'Truly, truly, I say to you, you seek Me, not because you saw signs, but because you ate of the loaves and were filled' " (John 6:26). He drew the people's attention to the reality that what He had done the day before was not just a miraculous provision of bread. It was a sign that was intended to teach something.

Then began an interesting exchange between Jesus and the people. They were trying to pin Him down and force Him to perform for them another miracle like the one He had done the day before. Jesus, for His part, was trying to reel them in and show them the true bread. Finally the people thought they had Him pinned, and they attempted to set the hook. " 'Lord, always give us this bread' " (John 6:34). Jesus then swept away the misconception and told them clearly, " 'I am the bread of life; he who comes to Me will not hunger, and he who believes in Me will never thirst' " (verse 35). Here the conversation began to fall apart. The people became aware that the food Jesus intended to give them was entirely different from the food they were looking for.

What It Means to Believe

Jesus continued to emphasize that those who believe in Him will not only have their hunger and thirst satisfied, but He will grant them eternal life. " 'Truly, truly, I say to you, he who believes has eternal life' " (John 6:47). One condition exists for gaining eternal life—we must believe in Jesus.

Some years ago I took a group of people rappelling at Ozone Falls in Tennessee. The cliffs there are overhanging, so after the first thirty feet of drop, the rock slopes away out of reach, and the one rappelling is suspended in midair, fully dependent on the rappelling equipment. That day, I clipped into the rope at the top of the cliff and prepared to back over the edge of the 150-foot drop to the jagged boulders below. At that point, the thought came forcefully into my mind that one small error in tying the anchor and my life would soon be over. I remember carefully checking my harness and anchor and connections. After checking everything carefully, I checked it all again! Of course, I am writing this chapter, so I must have done something right. However, if we as humans find it so important to make sure the anchor that protects our physical life is secure, how much more important it is to make sure that we have met the conditions for eternal life. The one condition is that we believe in Jesus. How important, then, that we understand what it means to believe!

When John recorded Jesus saying, " 'He who believes has eternal life,' " he tied eternal life with believing. Therefore, a better understanding of what *believing* meant to John can be deduced by comparing other passages where he described how to get eternal life. These texts provide evidence of what it means to believe.

Eternal life is found by . . .	Text
Believing in God's Son	John 3:16
Taking in the Holy Spirit	John 4:13, 14; 7:37–39
Hearing the words of Jesus and believing the One who sent Him	John 5:24
Doing what is good	John 5:28, 29
Coming to Jesus	John 5:39, 40
Eating Jesus' flesh and drinking His blood, that is, His Spirit, by internalizing His words	John 6:54–58, 63
Hearing Jesus' voice and following Him, like sheep following their shepherd	John 10:27, 28
Hating your life in this world; following and serving Jesus	John 15:25, 26
Hearing and keeping Jesus' sayings	John 12:44–50
Allowing Jesus to wash you	John 13:8

Knowing the Father and Jesus	John 17:3
Doing God's will	1 John 2:17
Having the Son	1 John 5:12
Being in the Father by being in His Son	1 John 5:20
Overcoming and keeping Jesus' deeds until the end	Revelation 2:7, 26

Through these texts, a clearer picture emerges of what John meant when he wrote, "He who believes has eternal life." The belief that leads to eternal life is one that involves internalizing Jesus' teachings. His words are alive—full of the Holy Spirit. When we take His words in, we take His Spirit in, and His Spirit then works marvelously within us to do all that He desires.

Many think that belief in Jesus amounts to a mere mental confidence that Jesus will grant us eternal life. Sadly, those who go no further than that are trusting in an anchor that will fail, plunging them to their eternal death. The consequences are far more disastrous than losing one's physical life here on earth.

In one of his letters, John described the Christian life as practicing righteousness. He said,

> No one who is born of God practices sin, because his seed abides in him; and he cannot sin, because he is born of God. By this the children of God and the children of the devil are obvious: anyone who does not practice righteousness is not of God, nor the one who does not love his brother (1 John 3:9, 10).

The practice of righteousness is like practicing the piano. Suppose a young girl begins taking piano lessons. The teacher assigns a very basic piece, and the child makes all sorts of mistakes. However, she keeps trying and eventually masters that piece. Then the teacher gives her a piece that is a little more difficult. The student at first makes all sorts of mistakes on that piece as well, but she eventually masters it too. If this process continues long enough, eventually she will play concert masterpieces flawlessly. The same is true in the Christian experience. When someone sets his heart to figure out God's will and do it, God reveals something that He wants that person to change. The person sets out to do it, but he struggles and fails, and then with God's help he eventually gets it right. Then God reveals another aspect of His will. At first the one practicing righteousness struggles and fails with that aspect as well, but eventually, with God's help, he gets it right too. If he continues in this process as long as life lasts, ever learning more of God's will, perhaps failing when initially applying it but getting back up and pressing on to get it right, God will grant him eternal life.

Following God means to head in the right direction. When I was a boy, I assembled a model rocket, painted it bright red, and stuffed the parachute down into the rather small cardboard tube that comprised the body. Excitedly I went with my family to a nearby clearing and prepared to launch it. Finally the moment came, and I pressed the button on the launcher. The rocket engine fired to life, and with a loud hiss, the rocket sailed into the sky. When the rocket reached the zenith, the engine was supposed to open the parachute with a small explosive blast, but the parachute was so tightly packed into the tube that it blew the rocket engine out of the back of the rocket. My heart sank as I watched the rocket turn downward. It plummeted toward the ground and, with a streak, disappeared behind some bushes. When we eventually found it among the weeds, only the fins were sticking out above the ground, and the rocket was ruined.

When the rocket was only inches off the launch pad and

headed skyward, there was far more hope for a successful flight than when it was 175 feet up and headed straight earthward. In a similar way, God's determination about our salvation does not hinge on our attaining a certain level of righteousness but rather on how set we are on finding His will and applying it in our lives. A right attitude is paramount—one of wholeheartedly seeking to know and do His will, depending on Him for strength to carry it out. The Ten Commandments, and any other list of laws, simply provides a framework upon which to build. One person can keep the form (the "letter") of the Ten Commandments and be headed straight earthward, so to speak, while another may not even fully understand the Ten Commandments, yet be completely set on finding out and implementing God's will.

The Food That Truly Satisfies

There by the sea, Jesus continued revealing the truth to the multitude. He said,

"I am the bread of life. Your fathers ate the manna in the wilderness, and they died. This is the bread which comes down out of heaven, so that one may eat of it and not die. I am the living bread that came down out of heaven; if anyone eats of this bread, he will live forever; and the bread also which I will give for the life of the world is My flesh" (John 6:48–51).

Jesus described Himself as the true bread out of heaven, something like the manna yet much greater.

Even the manna given to the Israelites in the wilderness was intended to teach an important lesson. It, too, was not just a miraculous provision of food. Moses said to the people,

"You shall remember all the way which the LORD your God has led you in the wilderness these forty years, that He might humble you, testing you, to know what was in your heart, whether you would keep His commandments or not. He humbled you and let you be hungry, and fed you with manna which you did not know, nor did your fathers know, that He might make you understand that man does not live by bread alone, but man lives by everything that proceeds out of the mouth of the LORD" (Deuteronomy 8:2, 3).

Just as the Israelites were sustained by the manna day after day, year after year, in the same way all people find true life by internalizing God's words day after day, year after year. The physical manna tasted like wafers with honey (Exodus 16:31); Jesus, in the form of His words, is the true manna, and all who will internalize His words will find that they are as sweet as honey.

Ezekiel had a vision of a scroll being given to him, and the scroll contained the words of God all over it. He was commanded to eat it, which he did, and he said that the scroll tasted like honey (Ezekiel 3:1–3). John had a similar experience. In vision he saw a mighty angel come down out of heaven who had a little book open in his hand. John was commanded to eat it, which he did, and he testified that it tasted as sweet as honey (Revelation 10:10). All who will take in Christ's teachings and apply them in their lives will find that they are as sweet as honey.

By this point, the discussion between Jesus and the people had deteriorated so much that the people were very disturbed. They began to argue with one another, saying, " 'How can this man give us His flesh to eat?' " (John 6:52). Jesus did not hold back, though. Winston Churchill once said to the future king of England, "If you have an important point to make, don't try to be subtle or clever. Use a pile driver. Hit the point once. Then come back and hit it again. Then hit it a third time, a tremendous whack." Here, Jesus did exactly that, hitting the point with terrific force, even though many in the audience were unwilling to accept it. His testimony stands today as a great light revealing the path that His followers should take. Jesus drove His point home, declaring, " 'Truly, truly, I say to you, unless you eat the flesh of the Son of Man and drink His blood, you have no life in yourselves' " (John 6:53). He did not say, "Figuratively, sort of, kind of," but rather, "Truly, truly." There is most definitely part of Jesus that we are to take in.

Jesus went on, " 'He who eats My flesh and drinks My blood has eternal life, and I will raise him up on the last day. For My flesh is true food, and My blood is true drink' " (John 6:54, 55). Food and drink can be defined as intake that supplies life. If this is so, then how much more could the intake that supplies eternal life be called food and drink? Which would you rather have, $70 or $1 million? In the same way, which is more important, the seventy or so years of this life or eternal life? Jesus' flesh and blood are the intake that supplies eternal life, and, therefore, is it not right to call them true food and drink?

When I was about four years old, we had a sandbox in our yard. One day I became curious about what sand tastes like, so I took a small handful and placed it in my mouth. To this day I can remember the surprising discovery that sand is tasteless and very crunchy. It rapidly spread between my teeth. Quickly I tried to spit it out. Even at four years old I berated myself for my lack of sense. That sand was not food. It provided no nutritional value. It did nothing to keep me healthy and strong, and it certainly was unpleasant. Our intake must provide energy and nutrients if it is to be considered food and drink.

Jesus said, " 'He who eats My flesh and drinks My blood abides in Me, and I in him' " (John 6:56). This statement is made up of two parts. The first part has to do with eating His flesh and drinking His blood. The second part has to do with abiding in Jesus and He in us. In other places Jesus taught how to abide in Him. These other texts provide parallels for the first part of Jesus' statement, where He talked about eating His flesh and drinking His blood. He said, " 'If you keep My commandments, you will abide in My love; just as I have kept My Father's commandments and abide in His love' " (John 15:10). And again, at another point John wrote about Jesus' teachings, saying, "The one who keeps His commandments abides in Him, and He in Him. We know by this that He abides in us, by the Spirit whom He has given us" (1 John 3:24). Abiding in Jesus therefore means that we keep His commandments. When Jesus made reference to eating His flesh and drinking His blood, what He meant was that we must keep His commandments.

Imagine I invite you over to my house to enjoy one of my wife's delicious meals. We gather around the dinner table, all set with dishes piled high with mashed potatoes, casserole, corn, salad, and fresh, homemade bread. After we fill our plates, we sit around the table for the next half hour, sniffing our food and complimenting my wife on the wonderful smells. We then rise from the table with our plates untouched and move into the living room to continue our conversation. Would that food profit us anything? No! It must go into our bodies and become part of us in order to do us any good. In the same way, Jesus' words must go into us and become part of us in order to do us any good.

One day Jesus met a blind man. He spat on the ground, made mud with the spittle, and then applied it to the man's eyes. He then gave him a command, saying, " 'Go, wash in the pool of Siloam' " (John 9:7). When the man went and washed, he gained his sight. What comes out of Jesus' mouth can cure our blindness, but for us to receive sight, when He applies His words to our lives, we must act on them. The blind man would not have been healed if he had not obeyed Jesus' command to wash.

After Jesus talked about eating His flesh and drinking His blood, many of His disciples said, " 'This is a difficult statement; who can listen to it?' " (John 6:60). However, Jesus left no doubt as to His meaning. He told them plainly, " 'It is the Spirit who gives life; the flesh profits nothing; the words that I have spoken to you are spirit and are life' " (verse 63). Jesus was not talking about His physical aspect, His flesh and blood. Yet He was most definitely talking about part of Himself—His Spirit. Jesus' words are different from mere human teaching. They are somehow alive, and when we internalize His words, we internalize His Spirit. His Spirit then dwells in us to give us the desire and ability to do whatever God wants.

Some have gotten the idea that at the Eucharist (communion), the bread and wine are somehow changed into Jesus' literal body and blood, and that by partaking of them, one somehow eats the flesh and drinks the blood of the Son of Man. Others, even if they do not go that far, think that at the communion service there is some special quality to the bread and grape juice that brings about a closer relationship with Jesus. However, in this text Jesus is abundantly clear that the physical part of Him counts for nothing. His physical flesh and blood do not provide life. It is His words that He considers to be His flesh and His blood. The Spirit brings life, and His Spirit is contained in His words. We eat Jesus' flesh and drink His blood by seeking out His teaching and acting on it.

For us to enter God's kingdom, two parts are required: God's part and our part. Our part is to adopt the all-important attitude: out of the love in our hearts for God we must seek to know and do His will, depending on Him for the strength to actually carry it out. God's part is, in response to our faith, to work in us to give us the desire and ability to fully comply with His will.

My wife has a large mixer that she uses to make bread and other food. The mixer has a cord that plugs into an electrical outlet. The cord by itself does nothing. Likewise, the electricity by itself does nothing. The cord must be plugged into the outlet, and then the electricity flows through the cord. Both are necessary for the machine to operate. Our part in the plan of salvation is like that cord. It has no power. It cannot of itself cause the machine to run. God's part is like the electricity. The electricity has all the power, but it cannot flow into the machine without the cord being connected to it. We must have God's power, but He must have our decision. If we decide to follow Him, depending on Him for strength, He will then work in us to will and to do according to His good pleasure.

Seeking to know and do God's will while depending on our own strength to carry it out is legalism. On the other hand, depending on God to grant us salvation without also seeking to know and do His will is what some have termed as cheap grace. Actually it is no grace at all, but rather presumption. We must have both parts—God's part and our part—in order to enter the kingdom of God.

Is there a nameless craving in your heart? Has your search for meaning left you with a desperate, empty feeling? Do you long for something to truly satisfy your heart? My friend, look no more. Let me recommend to you the Bible. It contains the words of God. Eat this word; drink it in and make it part of who you are. Don't be satisfied with just a crumb, but crave the whole plate. Don't stop with just a sip, but drink the whole pitcher. Read it in the morning when you wake up, listen to it on your phone as you go to and from work, memorize a passage during a break, read it to your children at family worship, think about it while you fall asleep, and above all, act on it. As we take in the words of God, we will find the true food and drink that satisfies the nameless craving in our hearts.

Discussion Questions:

1. When Jesus changed the water to wine, what are three things that the wine symbolized?

2. When Jesus changed one boy's lunch into a feast that fed a multitude, what did Jesus use that lunch to represent?

3. Jesus said, " 'He who believes has eternal life' " (John 6:47). Based on John's other writings that describe how to get eternal life, restate in your own words what Jesus meant by the word *believe*.

4. Explain what Jesus meant when He said, " 'Unless you eat the flesh of the Son of Man and drink His blood, you have no life in yourselves' " (John 6:53).

5. Jesus used signs and parables and illustrations to teach the concept that we must internalize His words in order to have life. Give your own example that illustrates this teaching.

6. List some things that we as humans pursue as though they would bring meaning, but ultimately leave us with a hunger that still remains.

7. This chapter discussed what it means to believe, emphasizing the writings of John. Compare these concepts with what Paul, Peter, and James said about belief. See Romans 3:20–31, 2 Peter 1:3–11, and James 2:14–26. What are the similarities and differences? How can the apparent differences be reconciled?

8. Jesus used the two great signs of wine and a lunch to illustrate the intake that truly satisfies. He taught the same lesson with the illustration of living water. Analyze Jesus' statements about that living water, and suggest one or two implications from them. See John 4:7–26 and John 7:37–39.

9. If unity with Christ is found by internalizing His words, what practical suggestions would you make for entering into a closer oneness with Him?

10. In what ways does Jesus' atonement for our sins have its basis in internalizing Jesus' words?

11. Compare and contrast legalism and presumption. Recommend ways to avoid both.

12. After evaluating the biblical evidence from this chapter, describe the standard for entering the kingdom of God.

CHAPTER TWO

A Place for You

In February of 2013, a California couple, identified only as John and Mary, were out walking their dog on their property, a route they had traveled many times before. Mary noticed an old rusty can protruding from the ground that had both ends still on it. John found a stick and poked around and scratched away the dirt until he freed the can from the soil.

Their curiosity was piqued as to what might be inside, so John picked up the can and began carrying it home. He commented to Mary, "Wow, this thing is heavy. It must be full of lead paint." Just about that time, one end of the can cracked open, and John caught a glimpse of the rim of a gold coin. Immediately it hit him that they had found something of immense value. John and Mary returned to the same spot and recovered seven more such cans. Altogether they contained 1,427 gold coins worth more than $10 million. The find has become known as the Saddle Ridge Hoard. It is believed to be the greatest buried treasure ever recovered in the United States.[2]

Judging by the dates on the coins, the treasure was buried in the late 1800s. For more than a hundred years it had lain in

---

2. "Interview," *Kagin's*, accessed Jan. 24, 2016, http://saddleridgehoard.com/interview/.

the dirt, moss growing on the cans, rust penetrating the walls, and mud seeping in among the coins. Through all that time, it went unnoticed and forgotten.

An even greater treasure has been almost obscured by the dust of time. The night before Jesus was crucified, He revealed the greatest message of love ever given to humanity. John 13:1 says, "Having loved His own who were in the world, He loved them to the end." The literal Greek interpretation is that He loved them to the uttermost, to the limit at which a thing ceases to be. In other words, He showed them the full extent of His love. It is time to raise this treasure from the dust and restore it to its true significance and its former glory.

As we glimpse the majesty of God's love, a great admiration and response of love awakens in our hearts. Our impurities become repulsive by contrast, and a passionate zeal forms within us to purify our own hearts so that Christ may perfectly dwell within us. In the first chapter we studied the food and drink that truly supply the nameless craving in our hearts. The only intake that provides meaning is the words of Jesus taken in and applied in one's life. Jesus' Spirit is embodied in His words, so when a person takes in His words, he is actually taking in Jesus' Spirit. The end result of taking in His Spirit is the greatest treasure of all time, namely, that if we have the Spirit of Jesus dwelling within us, Jesus then considers us as part of Himself, and, in turn, since Jesus and the Father are one, our unity with Jesus makes us one with the Father.

The prophets in the Old Testament predicted that Jesus would become a sanctuary for His people and they would be a sanctuary for Him. However, Jesus gave an even clearer description of this mystery the night before He was crucified. A concise summary of this treasure is encapsulated within John 14:2, 3. Let's spend this chapter carefully cleaning off each facet of this gemstone and arranging it properly with other gems of Scripture so that the glory of one makes the radiance of the others shine even brighter. If John 14:2, 3 could be expanded to include Jesus' intent behind the words, a paraphrase would sound something like this:

In My Father's house, which is the temple of My body, are many dwelling places—places for you to dwell in Me. If it were not so, I would have told you; many times in My teaching I have given you reason to believe that this could be true. If you had gotten the wrong idea, I would have corrected you. I go to the Father to experience the full measure of what it means to be in the Father, to prepare a place for you, so that you too may be in the Father. If I go and prepare a place for you, I will come again and receive you to myself, to be one with Me, so that where I am, in the Father, there you may also be.

Let's inspect this text phrase by phrase, uncovering the magnitude of its true meaning.

"In My Father's House . . ."

Jesus began by saying, "In My Father's house." Jesus Himself was His Father's house. Just a few verses beyond this passage, Jesus explains where His Father dwells. He said, " 'Do you not believe that I am in the Father, and the Father is in Me? The words that I say to you I do not speak on My own initiative, but the Father abiding in Me does His works' " (John 14:10). According to this passage, Jesus is the abiding place for the Father.

This idea was introduced in John 2, when Jesus found the money changers and merchants of animals in the temple courts engaging in commerce. He made a whip and drove them out, saying, " 'Take these things away; stop making My Father's house a place of business' " (verse 16). Here He identified the temple as His Father's house, but there was a deeper lesson He was trying to teach. The Jews came to Him and demanded, " 'What sign do You show us as Your authority for doing these things?' " (verse 18). In other words, "Show us evidence that You had permission to do what You just did."

Jesus answered them, " 'Destroy this temple, and in three days I will raise it up' " (verse 19).

The Jews mocked Him, saying, " 'It took forty-six years to build this temple, and will You raise it up in three days?' " However, John records in verse 21, "He was speaking of the temple of His body." Through this confrontation Jesus was trying to draw attention to the reality that His body was the true temple, the true house for His Father.

Some years ago, our family moved from Tennessee to California, and during the transition it took some time to finally sell our house back east. We decided to rent in California rather than own two properties. The house in Tennessee was ours, and the house in California belonged to our landlord. Occasionally we would invite family and friends or visitors from church to our house. Never once did any of them show up at our place in Tennessee, even though our claim of ownership was much stronger on that structure than on the house in California. Everyone understood that when we spoke of "our house," we were referring to the place where we resided. In like manner, the Father's house is the place where He resides. He resides in Jesus; therefore, Jesus is His Father's house.

". . . Are Many Dwelling Places"

Jesus continued His declaration to His disciples, saying, " 'In My Father's house are many dwelling places' " (John 14:2). He is not just a dwelling place for His Father. Here He reiterated that He is a dwelling place for all humans who believe in Him. John chapters 14 and 15 repeatedly emphasize a theme of abiding, and the full passage provides context for what Jesus meant when He spoke of many dwelling places in His

Father's house. Jesus said, " 'If anyone loves Me, he will keep My word; and My Father will love him, and We will come to him and make Our abode with him' " (John 14:23). The Greek word for abode in verse 23 is *μονή* (pronounced *monē)*, and it is the same as the word for dwelling place in verse 2. The King James Version translates verse 2 as, "In My Father's house are many mansions." If the same translation of *μονή* were used in verse 23 it would read, "If anyone loves Me, he will keep My word; and My Father will love him, and we will come to him and make our mansion with him." The mansions, or dwelling places, to which Jesus referred are dwelling places for us to dwell in Him and for Him to dwell in us.

Jesus continued in John 15:4, in the theme of abiding, " 'Abide in Me, and I in you. As the branch cannot bear fruit of itself unless it abides in the vine, so neither can you unless you abide in Me.' " Note that this text says that we are to abide, to dwell or reside, in Jesus. Jesus emphasized over and over in verses 5 through 9, "Abide . . . abide . . . abide in Me." In verse 10 He drove the point home, saying, " 'If you keep My commandments, you will abide in My love; just as I have kept My Father's commandments and abide in His love.' " Abiding is the result of internalizing Jesus' commands; it is the result of partaking of the true food and drink.

My computer is a laptop with Bluetooth capability. Sometimes I use a Bluetooth travel mouse. There is no mechanical connection between it and the computer, yet when I move the mouse, the cursor on the screen moves. Just the other day I took some pictures on my Bluetooth phone, then set it beside the computer and clicked the icon to connect it to the computer. The pictures soon popped up on my computer screen. The computer, mouse, and phone all work together as one system. There is no mechanical connection between them, yet they operate together as a unit. In similar fashion, those who become one with Jesus are separate from Him in physical body yet connected with Him in Spirit and operating as one with Him.

Paul referred to this mystery when he wrote, "Now to Abraham and his seed were the promises made. He saith not, And to seeds, as of many; but as of one, And to thy seed, which is Christ" (Galatians 3:16, KJV). As previously mentioned, the word *seed* is singular, not plural. The promises were given to one, and only one, of Abraham's descendants. The text emphasizes that the one descendant spoken about was Christ.

Later in the same chapter, Paul revealed a stunning insight.

For ye are all the children of God by faith in Christ Jesus. For as many of you as have been baptized into Christ have put on Christ. There is neither Jew nor Greek, there is neither bond nor free, there is neither male nor female: for ye are all one in Christ Jesus. And if ye be Christ's, then are *ye* Abraham's *seed*, and heirs according to the promise (Galatians 3:26–29, KJV, italics supplied).

When we are baptized into Christ, we put on Christ and become part of that one and only seed to whom the promises were given.

When God gave the promises to Abraham and his seed, He embedded in those promises a figure of the reality to come. God told Abraham to sacrifice his only son Isaac as a burnt offering on a mountain in Moriah. Abraham obeyed, and he would have killed his son except that God intervened at the last moment. Then God spoke.

"By myself have I sworn," saith the LORD, "for because thou hast done this thing, and hast not withheld thy son, thine only son: that in blessing I will bless thee, and in multiplying I will multiply thy seed as the stars of the heaven, and as the sand which is upon the sea shore; and thy seed shall possess the gate of his enemies; and in thy seed shall all the nations of the earth be blessed; because thou hast obeyed my voice" (Genesis 22:16–18, KJV).

God told Abraham that his seed (singular) would be like the stars of the heaven. In other words, this one individual would be composed of many parts. Then He gave a different illustration, saying that Abraham's seed would be like the sand of the seashore, made up of many individuals. Just as Abraham offered his only son as a burnt offering on a mountain in Moriah, and then the promises regarding this unique seed were given, in a similar manner God sent His only Son Jesus as a sacrifice for us. He died on a mountain in Moriah, and He fulfilled the promise about the seed by opening a way for people to become part of that one true seed.

When I was a child, my parents sometimes pulled out a candelabrum on special occasions. The candelabrum had several branches. They would place candles in it and light them, and the branches would hold up those candles to shed light over the whole table. That one candelabrum can be compared to Jesus. It was made up of one piece, but that one unit had multiple branches, each one holding up a shining light. In similar fashion, Jesus is one, but He has many branches, each one holding the Holy Spirit within it.

This mystery was foreshadowed all the way back in the Garden of Eden. God told Adam and Eve, " 'From the tree of the knowledge of good and evil you shall not eat, for in the day that you eat from it you will surely die' " (Genesis 2:17). Interestingly, on the day that they ate from that tree, they did not die. However, something did die, because God clothed Adam and Eve with skins, and then they were allowed to live on. The passage in Galatians points out that as many as are baptized into Christ have put on Christ. They put Him on in the same way Adam and Eve put on the skins of those animals in the garden. By putting on Christ, they become one with Him, and then His death can count for them. They are then allowed to live on.

Referring again to the symbolism in the Garden of Eden, it could be said that symbolically Adam and Eve did die on the day they ate from that tree, because they were clothed with the skins of those animals, thus figuratively becoming one with the animals. Symbolically the death of those animals was their own death, since they were figuratively one with them. Since they figuratively died, the punishment was satisfied, and they were allowed to live on. Now, it was only a symbol, and Adam and Eve eventually did die, but all who put on Christ are granted life that will never end. Even if they do die in this age, God will grant them immortality at the resurrection.

Jesus alluded to this oneness in His conversation with Nicodemus. In one of the most quoted passages of Scripture He said, " 'For God so loved the world, that He gave His only begotten Son, that whoever believes in Him shall not perish, but have eternal life' " (John 3:16). According to this text, God has one and only one son. How, then, can you and I be called children of God? How can God have only one Son, yet have many sons? John began his book by writing, "In the beginning was the Word, and the Word was with God, and the Word was God" (John 1:1). A few verses later He revealed how it is that we can be called children of God: "But as many as received him, to them gave he power to become the sons of God, even to them that believe on his name" (verse 12, KJV). The "Him" mentioned in this passage is the Word. We are to believe in His name. What is His name? The Word. Just as we touched on in chapter 1, Jesus is embodied in a set of teachings, and when we take in Jesus' words and apply them in our lives, we are taking Jesus in—we are receiving Him. He is "God with us." When we become part of the Son of God, we then gain the right to be called children of God, since He Himself is God's child.

A distinction exists between us and Jesus, yet our unity with Him is so close that we can be considered one. We are one in Spirit, which results in our becoming one with Him in mind, in purpose, and in character. Our physical bodies are distinct, but we share the same Spirit. The unity Jesus has with the Father is an exact example of the relationship that Jesus wants us to have with Himself. Jesus and the Father are distinct individuals. Each has his own physical body and is his own entity. Jesus said, " 'The Son can do nothing of Himself' " (John 5:19). If He and the Father were one individual, He would have said, "The Son can do everything of Himself." On the cross Jesus prayed to His Father, saying, " 'Into Your hands I commit My spirit.' " He was not committing His Spirit into the care of a man who would be dead in a few moments but into the hands of another individual who was still alive.

While Jesus and the Father are distinct in their physical persons, yet they are still one. Philip asked Jesus to show them the Father. Jesus replied, " 'Have I been so long with you, and yet you have not come to know Me, Philip? He who has seen Me has seen the Father; how can you say, "Show us the Father"?' " (John 14:9). Jesus was so close to the Father that it could be said that if you have seen Jesus, you have seen the Father. Paul likened this unity to that of a husband and wife. He wrote,

> Husbands ought also to love their own wives as their own bodies. He who loves his own wife loves himself; for no one ever hated his own flesh, but nourishes and cherishes it, just as Christ also does the church, because we are members of his body. For this reason a man shall leave his father and mother and shall be joined to his wife, and the two shall become one flesh. This mystery is great (Ephesians 5:28–32a).

And then Paul turned the discussion on its head, saying, "But I am speaking with reference to Christ and the church" (verse 32b). Those who take in Christ's teaching become one flesh with Him. He was not talking about the physical aspects of Him, but He was most definitely talking about part of Him—His Spirit.

Do you not know that your bodies are members of Christ? Shall I then take away the members of Christ and make them members of a prostitute? May it never be! Or do you not know that the one who joins himself to a prostitute is one body with her? For He says, "The two shall become one flesh." But the one who joins himself to the Lord is one spirit with Him (1 Corinthians 6:15–17).

In a marriage the two become one flesh physically. With respect to Christ, a believer becomes one flesh with Him in Spirit.

Jesus considers us one with Himself if His Spirit is dwelling within us. A dangerous counterfeit says God is within all. A Hindu friend once told me, "God is within you and me and everyone." Sadly, my friend is caught in a deception of Satan that is designed to lead away from the true reality. According to the texts we have been studying, God is not within all. He is only within those who take in His word and act on it.

While God is not within all, Jesus did go so far as to call them gods to whom the word of God comes. What does it mean for the word of God to come to someone? It means that that person internalizes God's words, as we have been studying. Jesus claimed to be the Son of God, and the Jews picked up rocks to stone Him for blasphemy. In this claim they understood Him to be making Himself equal with God. In the defense Jesus gave, He reveals the level to which God will exalt those who follow Him. He told the Jews,

"Has it not been written in your Law, 'I said, you are gods'? If He called them gods, to whom the word of God came (and the Scripture cannot be broken), do you say of Him, whom the Father sanctified and sent into the world, 'You are blaspheming, because I said, 'I am the Son of God'?" (John 10:34–37).

Those who wholeheartedly obey His teachings, Jesus

considers to be gods. They do not become autonomous, self-reliant gods who share equal authority with Jesus and the Father, but rather they are part of Jesus and fully under His authority.

God spoke through Isaiah this way:

"Before Me there was no God formed, and there will be none after Me. I, even I, am the Lord, and there is no savior besides Me. It is I who have declared and saved and proclaimed, and there was no strange god among you; so you are My witnesses," declares the Lord, "and I am God" (Isaiah 43:10–12).

Only one God exists. According to Isaiah, there has only ever been and will only ever be one God. All other so-called gods are false gods. Therefore, if those who internalize Jesus' words are to be truly called gods, the only way is for them to be part of the one true God. We are not gods in and of ourselves. In fact, Jesus said, " 'Apart from Me you can do nothing' " (John 15:5). A believer's only claim to that title is that God is dwelling in that person in the form of His Holy Spirit.

There is a heavenly hierarchy of authority. Jesus was granted all authority by His Father. Since it is the Father who granted Jesus that authority, it is self-evident that the Father has higher authority than Jesus. (See 1 Corinthians 15:27, 28.) At the company where I work there is an organizational structure. The chief executive officer has the greatest authority, and under him are several other executive officers, and in turn under them are the rest of the employees. In spiritual terms, the Father could be compared to the CEO, Jesus could be compared to the other executive officers, and Jesus' followers to the rest of the employees. The mechanism whereby we can be called gods, or more descriptively, sons of God, is that we take in the Son of God by internalizing His teaching. This mechanism automatically places us in subjection to His authority. To become a subject of this kingdom, we must be subject to its King. When we are subject to Him, following His words and obeying Him, then He welcomes us into the kingdom, into one of the many dwelling places in Himself.

"If It Were Not So, I Would Have Told You"

Jesus continued, "'If it were not so, I would have told you'" (John 14:2). He often taught about this subject. During His ministry Jesus had already given people many reasons to believe that it might be possible to dwell in Him. He affirmed that if it were not possible to dwell in Him, and His disciples had started getting the wrong ideas, He would have corrected them.

In chapter 1 we talked about two great signs Jesus gave to teach this lesson, first when He changed the water to wine, and second when He turned one boy's lunch into a feast for a whole multitude. He alluded to this same subject when He spoke to the woman at the well, telling her, " 'Whoever drinks of the water that I will give him shall never thirst; but the water that I will give him will become in him a well of water springing up to eternal life' " (John 4:14). This water satisfies the thirst in our hearts. He again spoke of it at the Feast of Tabernacles, standing up on the last day of the feast and crying out, " 'If anyone is thirsty, let him come to Me and drink. He who believes in Me, as the Scripture said, "From his innermost being will flow rivers of living water" ' " (John 7:37, 38). In goes a sip, out comes a river; in goes a little of his Spirit when we take in his words, out comes a river of obedience born from his Spirit dwelling within.

Jesus compared Himself in John 10 to a door for the sheep. He did not say that He was the doorkeeper, pointing the way to eternal life. Rather, He emphasized that He Himself was the door. " 'I am the door of the sheep. . . . If anyone enters through Me, he will be saved' " (John 10:7, 9). Only through Jesus may we enter into life; we must become part of him.

The book of John was written for two purposes, first, "that you may believe that Jesus is the Christ, the Son of God," and second, "that believing you may have life in His name" (20:31). John held very closely to these two themes when he penned the Gospel that bears his name. A worthwhile study is to go through the book and identify which texts serve the first purpose and which texts serve the second. We cannot look in detail at all these texts here, but such a study helps reveal a clearer picture of what it means to have life in Jesus' name. To this teaching Jesus referred when He said, " 'If it were not so, I would have told you.' "

Five months after I started a new job in Tennessee, I had my first performance review. Up to that point my boss had given me great autonomy when working on my project, and I enjoyed the independence and ability to run the project as I thought best. At the same time, I wondered how my boss felt about my performance. Was he just giving me space to get acclimated to the new role but was not happy with my efforts? At the performance review I brought up this topic. He quickly assured me, "Oh, I was watching to make sure you were on track. If you had gone off course, I would have reined you back in." In like manner Jesus assured His disciples that He would have redirected them had they developed wrong ideas: " 'If it were not so, I would have told you.' "

"I Go to Prepare a Place for You"

Jesus continued to unveil this mystery to His disciples. He told them, " 'I go to prepare a place for you.' " The place Jesus spoke of preparing was a place for us in Himself and ultimately a place for us in the Father. A few verses later, He reveals where He will dwell ultimately, and where His followers will dwell. " 'In that day you will know that I am in My Father, and you in Me, and I in you' " (John 14:20). Jesus was going to dwell in the Father, and His followers are going to dwell in Jesus.

Now to be clear, there is ample evidence from other Bible passages that there is a literal heaven and a physical city, the New Jerusalem. In heaven, God will more than adequately meet all of our physical needs. But this is not what Jesus was emphasizing in John 14:2, 3. He was not here saying that He was going to heaven to build physical mansions for us. He who created the heavens and the earth in six days did not need two thousand years, or 700,000 days, to create a mere city. He could simply speak it into existence in a day. Besides, the disciples left their houses and camped out in the elements just so they could be near Jesus, proving that they counted His presence more dear than physical shelter. Did Jesus really think that they would prefer to have a fine mansion in a few thousand years rather than continuing to bask in His presence? Who among us would not be thrilled to even camp under a shrub in heaven just to be near Jesus? Who needs a physical city if we have Jesus? When Jesus said He was going to prepare a place for us, He was not saying He had to solve a housing shortage in heaven before He could take us to dwell there.

It was necessary for Jesus to prepare a place in Himself for us, otherwise He could not justly pay for our sins. God revealed to Ezekiel His sense of justice, saying,

> "The person who sins will die. The son will not bear the punishment for the father's iniquity, nor will the father bear the punishment for the son's iniquity; the righteousness of the righteous will be upon himself, and the wickedness of the wicked will be upon himself" (Ezekiel 18:20).

In God's system of justice, only the one who commits the sin can justly pay for it.

This notion is the same in our western legal system. Suppose someone steals a car. The police open an investigation, nab a suspect, and convict him, and he goes to jail. After five years they realize there has been a terrible mistake—they got the wrong guy. They release the innocent man, reopen the investigation, and this time they get the right guy. At his sentencing, will the judge decrease the time he has to serve because of the time the innocent man already served? No indeed. Only the person who committed the crime can justly pay for it. So it is with God. Jesus could only justly pay for His own sins; therefore, in order to pay for our sins, He had to make us one with Himself so that our sins became His sins.

When the Father caused the guilt of our iniquities to fall on Jesus, it was to the degree that those iniquities were considered as belonging to Jesus. David prophesied in Psalm 40,

> Sacrifice and meal offering You have not desired; my ears You have opened; burnt offering and sin offering You have not required. Then I said, "Behold, I come; in the scroll of the book it is written of Me. I delight to do Your will, O my God; Your Law is within my heart" (verses 6–8).

(Hebrews 10:4–10 specifically applies this prophecy to Jesus.) Psalm 40 continues in the next verses with a description of Jesus' manner of preaching. However, in verses 11 and 12 the tone changes.

> You, O LORD, will not withhold Your compassion from me; Your lovingkindness and Your truth will continually preserve me. For evils beyond number have surrounded me; my iniquities have overtaken me, so that I am not able to see; they are more numerous than the hairs of my head, and my heart has failed me.

Jesus was sinless, but the prophet, speaking from Jesus' perspective, here speaks as though He is sinful. When the Father placed our sins upon Jesus, Jesus then claimed our sins as His own.

God illustrated this concept to the Israelites. Because of

their rebellion He sent venomous snakes among them, and some of the people were bitten and died. Then God told Moses to make a bronze snake and hang it on a pole. Any who were bitten and then looked at the bronze snake would be cured. Jesus referred to this illustration during His ministry, saying, " 'As Moses lifted up the serpent in the wilderness, even so must the Son of man be lifted up' " (John 3:14). In the Scriptures the snake is a symbol of Satan and of evil. Jesus was to become one with us, taking our sin, our evil, upon Himself to the degree that it was considered His own, so that He could pay for the guilt of our transgressions. In turn, by His making us one with Himself, we can become pure and righteous, as He Himself is righteous. Paul wrote, "He made Him who knew no sin to be sin on our behalf, so that we might become the righteousness of God in Him" (2 Corinthians 5:21).

"If I Go and Prepare a Place for You, I Will Come Again and Receive You to Myself"

Jesus assured His disciples that He would come back again and receive them to Himself. This promise is more than a pledge to bring His disciples in close physical proximity to where He dwells. He is going to receive His disciples into the full experience of what it means to dwell in Him.

Jesus came to John on the Isle of Patmos and gave him a message for the seven churches in Asia Minor, which were representative of His church in all ages. To the church in Philadelphia He promised, " 'He who overcomes, I will make him a pillar in the temple of my God, and he will not go out from it anymore' " (Revelation 3:12). We have already studied how Jesus was the temple for the Father. If there is any remaining doubt as to what it means to be pillars in the temple, John clarified what the temple is when he described the New Jerusalem coming down out of heaven. He wrote, "I saw no temple in it, for the Lord God the Almighty and the Lamb are its temple" (Revelation 21:22). There is a temple in heaven now, for Revelation speaks of it several times. However, in the future, at the time when the churches will be enjoying the rewards of overcoming, there will be no temple other than the Lord God the Almighty and the Lamb. The overcomers will become pillars in the temple composed of the Lord God the Almighty and the Lamb.

We have not yet experienced the full measure of what God has planned for us, but He gave us the Holy Spirit as a down payment, guaranteeing the good things to come. Jesus said, " 'It is for your good that I go away, for unless I go away the Comforter will not come to you.' " Jesus promised His disciples,

> "I will ask the Father, and He will give you another helper, that He may be with you forever; that is the Spirit of truth, whom the world cannot receive, because it does not see Him or know Him, but you know Him because He abides with you and will be in you" (John 14:16, 17).

Note that at the time Jesus spoke these words, the Holy Spirit was only abiding "with" the disciples, but in the next phrase Jesus promised that at some future point He would be "in" them. On the one hand, at the time Jesus spoke these words, the Holy Spirit was already active in the world, providing guidance, comfort, and instruction. Moreover, He was present everywhere, so in one sense He already was in the disciples because He occupied the same physical space that they occupied. On the other hand, the believers' relationship to the Holy Spirit changed so dramatically after Jesus was raised that John says the Holy Spirit was not even given until that time (John 7:39). Also, even though the Spirit was already with the disciples, Jesus said the Comforter could not come unless Jesus went to the Father (John 16:7). Finally, even though the Spirit physically occupied the same space as the believers, Jesus did not consider the Spirit to be "in" them until after Jesus was glorified. Therefore there must be a greater meaning when Jesus said that the Holy Spirit "is with you and *will be in you*." The change that occurred was that now the Holy Spirit becomes part of Jesus' followers, rather than being a separate entity.

Several years ago, my wife and I visited the Cape Hatteras lighthouse on North Carolina's Outer Banks. During the day, the light from the sun illuminates the structure, and people many miles away can recognize the distinctive black-and-white daymark pattern painted on its surface. However, when night falls, no external illumination can penetrate the darkness out over Diamond Shoals, a deadly twelve-mile-long sandbar lying just underwater a few miles off the coast. It is then that an internal light is required, inside the lighthouse, one positioned at just the right spot within the large Fresnel lens. The lens pieces bend the light and focus it into a concentrated beam that flashes its warning to sailors far out on the sea, guiding them safely past the infamous Graveyard of the Atlantic. These two types of illumination illustrate the work of the Holy Spirit before and after Jesus was glorified. Before Jesus was glorified, the Holy Spirit was with us, like the external light from the sun illuminating the lighthouse. After Jesus was glorified, the Holy Spirit became part of us, like the light blazing within the Fresnel lens.

"That Where I Am . . ."

In my earlier Christian experience, I read Jesus' statement, "That where I am," and simply assumed He was referring to heaven. However, in the book of John, not once did John ever say that Jesus was going to heaven. Time and again He drove home the point that Jesus was going to the Father. While it may not be wrong to say that Jesus was going to heaven, the statement is incomplete. He was not just going to heaven, He was going to a very specific destination.

In the very next verse Jesus said,

"And you know the way where I am going." Thomas said to Him, "Lord, we do not know where You are going, how do we know the way?" Jesus said to him, "I am the way, and the truth, and the life; no one comes *to the Father* but through Me" (John 14:4–6, italics supplied).

When asked where He was going, Jesus here indicated that He was going to the Father. Later that evening He stated it again: " 'But now I am going to Him who sent Me; and none of you asks Me, "Where are You going?" ' " (John 16:5). And if that were not enough, He said it a third time: " 'I came forth from the Father and have come into the world; I am leaving the world again and going to the Father' " (verse 28). He was going to a very specific destination.

If I tell someone, "The family and I are going to visit the White House," it would not be wrong for that individual to tell someone else, "Their family is going to Washington D.C." However, their statement would be incomplete. The story has more detail to it; our family is going to a very specific destination within Washington D.C. Similarly, Jesus was going to a very specific destination in heaven—to the Father.

". . . There You May Also Be"

John 14:3 concludes with Jesus saying, " 'That where I am, there you may also be.' " Jesus was going to the Father to experience the full measure of what it means to be in the Father. We also may be in that same destination. John wrote, "And we know that the Son of God has come, and has given us understanding so that we may know Him who is true; and we are in Him who is true, in His Son Jesus Christ. This is the true God and eternal life" (1 John 5:20). The Father is referred to in this text as "Him who is true." The text brings out that we are in the Father by being in His Son, Jesus Christ.

A church building contains a sanctuary within it. In turn,

the sanctuary contains seats within it. If the seats are part of the sanctuary, and the sanctuary is part of the church building, then the seats are also part of the church building. Believers are like those seats, Jesus is like the sanctuary, and the Father is like the church building. If believers are part of Jesus and Jesus is part of the Father, then believers are part of the Father as well. This is the mystery to which Jesus directed His disciples when He said, " 'Where I am, there you may also be.' "

In this chapter we have studied the staggering promises Jesus gave when He revealed to His disciples the full extent of His love. If you have not already done so, will you make this treasure yours right now? Look at the astonishing benefits of becoming one with Christ. First, in this life we have the comfort of the Holy Spirit. Second, when we face death we have the hope that by becoming one with Christ, we participate with Him not only in His death but also in His resurrection. Third, in the life to come we will sit down with Christ on His throne, just as He overcame and sat down with His Father on His throne. We will rule the nations with a rod of iron, even as Jesus received authority from His Father. We will experience deep fellowship with both the Father and the Son. The $10 million Saddle Ridge Hoard seems like a particle of rubbish in comparison.

Only one condition exists for receiving this treasure—we must adopt the all-important attitude described in chapter 1. We must eat the words of Jesus. You may have partaken of His words for many years, or you may still be trying to make it a reality in your life. If you are struggling to make a full surrender of yourself to God, do not despair. You are not alone in your battle. He who cleared the temple is consumed with zeal for His Father's house. Go to Him all stained and corrupt as you are. Ask Him to help you, and He will zealously drive out anything within you that hinders fellowship with Him and the Father. Determine in your mind to wholeheartedly figure out and perform whatever God desires you to do, all the while recognizing that you have no strength in you to make it a reality. Ask God for His supernatural strength to obey Him, and He will help you. Do not let another day pass without securing this treasure for yourself. It is the greatest treasure of all time.

Discussion Questions:

1. Who is the temple for the Father?

2. What was the place Jesus was going to prepare for His followers?

3. Explain how Jesus was God's only Son, yet we too can be called sons of God.

4. In your own words, describe what Jesus meant when He said, " 'In My Father's house are many dwelling places. If it were not so I would have told you. I go to prepare a place for you, and if I go and prepare a place for you I will come again and receive you to Myself, that where I am, there you may be also.' "

5. Several times Jesus illustrated the concept of the unity we can have with Him. He described it as branches being united to the vine, as eating His flesh and drinking His blood, and as a drink that turns into a spring of water flowing from within us. Based on the information from this present chapter, give your own illustration of what it means to be one with Christ.

6. Draw a timeline showing the development of oneness with Christ, including the Holy Spirit being with us, the Holy Spirit being in us, and the ultimate unity with Jesus and the Father. Explain your reasoning.

7. According to John 20:31 the gospel of John was written for two purposes: first, "that you might know

that Jesus is the Christ, the Son of God," and second, "that by believing you may have life in His name." Select a couple of the chapters from John and discuss which parts bear witness that Jesus is the Christ, the Son of God, and which parts teach what it means to have life in His name.

8. In chapter 1 we studied how when a person internalizes Jesus' words, that person takes in Jesus' Spirit. Then in the present chapter we studied the outcome of internalizing His Spirit. Since it is so important to take in His Spirit, what if our resolve fails and we sin? Why do some people such as King Saul fall and never rise again, and other people such as King David fall but then regain a close relationship with God?

9. Read the passage in 1 Kings 8:23–61 that records Solomon's dedication prayer for the temple. Just as Solomon was the son of David who built the earthly temple, Jesus was the son of David who built the true temple. In what ways could Solomon's dedicatory prayer be applied to our relationship with Jesus?

10. Read some of the promises given to the "seed" of Abraham, Isaac, and Jacob (Genesis 15:12–18; 17:1–9; 21:12; 28:13–15; 35:10–12). How is our understanding of these passages affected when we recognize that Jesus is the one seed and His followers become part of that seed by becoming one with Christ?

11. Based on the information in the present chapter and your own study, deduce what it means to be one with the Father. Describe to the rest of the class your inferences.

12. Not only did Jesus cleanse the temple and use it as a living illustration of how He is His Father's house, but

in the process He also revealed the way that He treats those who become part of Himself. He vehemently drives out anything within them that hinders unity with Him. What things in your life need to be driven out so that your unity with Him will not be hindered?

CHAPTER THREE

Jesus Is Our Example

My second job out of college was working for a manufacturer of electromagnetic components. We made motion control devices for a number of aerospace applications and other uses. My supervisor was a man named John, and he was a licensed Professional Engineer. In order to get that licensure, he had to have at least a bachelor's degree in engineering. Then he had to take the Fundamentals of Engineering exam, an eight-hour-long assessment testing the theoretical aspects of engineering. On top of that, he had to have at least four years of work experience. Two years of that work experience had to be under another licensed Professional Engineer. Finally he had to take the Professional Engineering exam, which was another eight-hour-long assessment testing the practical aspects of engineering.

John had made it through all of that and obtained his licensure. He was very good at what he did. When I went to work at that company, he began training me and helping me learn how to do engineering the way he did engineering. He taught me electromagnetics, he gave me all the calculations and the tables that he used, and he mentored me in computer-aided design applications. He taught me about due diligence, making sure that what I was doing was thorough and complete. After a couple of years of him mentoring me, my engineering started to look a whole lot like his engineering. In fact, to this day, years later, the way I do engineering has been greatly influenced by John.

In a similar way, when we become disciples of Christ, Jesus becomes our mentor and we are mentees under Him. We learn from Him. He teaches us His ways. And the longer we are under His training, the more our actions look like His.

The first two chapters of this book dealt with the unity God wants us to have with Him. But questions arise. In practical terms, what does it mean to be part of God? What does it not mean? Most important of all, how can we enter into the experience God offers us without stepping into error?

Jesus is our example in this area. The night before He was crucified, He prayed, " 'I do not ask on behalf of these alone,' " meaning His eleven remaining disciples, " 'but for those also who believe in Me through their word; that they may all be one; even as You, Father, are in Me and I in You, that they also may be in us, so that the world may believe that You sent Me' " (John 17:20, 21). Therefore the unity He wants us to have with Him is patterned after the unity He has with the Father.

That brings us to the main idea I would like us to take away: the unity Jesus has with the Father is a model of the unity He wants us to have with Him, which includes the following five areas: (1) the intimacy He has with the Father, (2) the works He does, (3) His suffering, (4) His resurrection, and (5) His glory.

Two Dangers

Two dangers exist against which we must guard. The first danger is that a shallow understanding could lead people to be deceived by eastern religions, even though in reality this doctrine is diametrically opposed to those religious beliefs. Raindrops falling just one foot apart on the continental divide will end up in separate oceans. In a similar way, at first glance, the distinction between God's truth and certain eastern religions seems subtle. Both speak of being one with God. But below the surface, vast differences emerge. Many say that God is within all, when in reality He is only within those who wholeheartedly internalize His teachings. Many seek for experiences with wonderful feelings, and they base their decisions of right and wrong on whether they experience those feelings. However, God wants us to choose what is right and wrong based on His teachings, regardless of how we feel. Many adopt mystic practices for approaching God that depend on emptying the mind of all thought so that they can "hear" God or experience Him in the silence, while the true way to draw close to God is to internalize His words that are plainly taught in the Bible.

The key question is one of authority. Who is in charge of your life? You or Jesus? If a person believes that he innately possesses divinity, then there is no need for him to surrender to Christ. He believes he is already a god, and as such his choices are as good as God's verdicts. Therefore he becomes his own highest authority. Likewise, if a person relies on his own feelings rather than the Word of God, that person sets himself up as his own highest authority. Be on your guard against the notion that all people innately possess divinity. Be on your guard against the concept that unsubstantiated impressions are a trustworthy guide. Following such ideas will ruin your Christian experience. The true Christian experience leads to complete submission to God. Based on the all-important attitude described in chapter 1, it is a mindset of wholeheartedly seeking to know and do God's will, depending on Him for the strength to make the necessary changes.

The second danger related to this subject is that in our efforts to distance ourselves from the perils of eastern religions, we will reject the Bible's teaching on unity with God. The only safe course is to base our beliefs on a careful study of the Scriptures, no matter how similar or dissimilar the truth may be to any other belief system. If we reject the truth because deadly errors lie close to it, we still reject the truth! And the consequences of rejecting truth are extreme. God is extending a great offer of fellowship to you and me. How can we reject Him by failing to believe in the gift He wants to share with us? It would be like a girlfriend declining her boyfriend's marriage proposal just because she felt his desire for such a deep relationship with her was too wonderful to be true. And worse yet, if we classify truth with error, then we could end up opposing the very ones who are following the truth, thus effectively putting ourselves into Satan's army, fighting against the very God we profess to love.

The Problem of Oversimplification

Many have tried to describe unity with God, and some have attempted to simplify the subject to a few one-word terms. But I fear that so doing oversimplifies the subject to the point that the true biblical sense of unity with God becomes indiscernible. Albert Einstein once said, "The supreme goal of all theory is to make the irreducible basic elements as simple and as few as possible without having to surrender the adequate representation of a single datum of experience."[3] What he meant was, "Make things as simple as possible, but not simpler." I am all for simplifying ideas so that they are easily understandable, but it is possible to simplify them to the point that they lose the detail that brings clarity. Have you ever taken a low-resolution picture and later zoomed in on it, only to realize that the image was grainy and pixilated, lacking the clarity to see what you wanted to see? The same holds true if

---

3. Albert Einstein, "On the Method of Theoretical Physics," The Herbert Spencer Lecture, delivered at Oxford University, June 10, 1933; published in *Philosophy of Science* 1, no. 2 (April 1934), 163–169.

we oversimplify the subject of unity with God. The Bible gives many detailed descriptions of what oneness with God really constitutes. If we put the clues together, a high-resolution image emerges that provides a clear picture of that unity. Let's start unpacking those clues.

Jesus Is Our Example in His Intimacy with the Father

The first of the five areas where Jesus is our example is the intimacy He has with the Father. When we try to grasp the intimacy believers can have with Jesus, it is helpful to realize that such intimacy is a carbon copy of the intimacy Jesus has with the Father. One aspect of that intimacy is the love they have with one another. Jesus said in John 15:9, " 'Just as the Father has loved Me, I have also loved you.' " The level of love that the Father and Son share, we can share with Jesus.

When I was growing up, my father expressed his love to me in numerous ways. He was a very hard worker, and he provided well for his family, even though he did not make a lot of money. We never lacked any essential thing. He also spent time with us, going camping or snow skiing or hiking. And he made it a point to regularly hug us and tell us he loved us. Time has passed, and now I am a father with four children, and in order to express my love for them I find myself doing the same things my dad did: taking them on special outings, making sure they are provided for, and hugging them and telling them that I love them. The love my father shared with me is the same quality of love that I now pass on to my children. With God it is similar. The love the Father gave to Jesus is the love Jesus then gives to you and to me.

The second aspect of the intimacy they share is their name. John 17:11 says, " 'I am no longer in the world; and yet they themselves are in the world, and I come to You. Holy Father, keep them in Your name, the name which You have given Me, that they may be one even as We are.' " When we are called by His name, it is much more than just assuming a name change. You can call an orange a banana, but that does not make it a banana. However, with Jesus, when we are called by His name, we become part of Him in a way such that the orange does become a banana, so to speak.

Jesus' name is like that of a city. When Chicago was founded in 1837, it covered ten square miles. Over the following decades, areas surrounding Chicago were added to the city, and they became part of it. In one annexation in 1889, 125 square miles was added at one time. By the turn of the century, the city limits encompassed 180 square miles. When those areas were annexed and became part of Chicago, it was not just in name. They became part of Chicago in order to take advantage of the economies of scale. They became entitled to the services—police departments, utilities, fire departments, trash pickup, and so on. The surrounding areas desired to become part of Chicago due to the lower cost for having these services. Of course, they also shared in paying the taxes, which was the other aspect of joining the city. Nevertheless, they became part of Chicago not just in name but in function. They were one. And they operated as one unit.[4] It is the same way with Jesus and the Father. The Father annexed Jesus, so to speak. They became one unit, operating as one entity. In like manner, when Jesus makes us one with Himself, He "annexes" us. We become part of who He is. This intimacy that Jesus has with the Father is a perfect model for us of the intimacy He wants us to have with Him.

A third aspect in which His intimacy is a model for us is in the Holy Spirit. At Jesus' baptism the Holy Spirit came down in bodily form. John the Baptist testified, saying,

---

4. The Encyclopedia of Chicago, s.v. "Annexation." Chicago Historical Society, 2005, http://www.encyclopedia.chicagohistory.org /pages/53.html.

"I have seen the Spirit descending as a dove out of heaven, and He remained upon Him. I did not recognize Him, but He who sent me to baptize in water said to me, 'He upon whom you see the Spirit descending and remaining upon Him, this is the one who baptizes in the Holy Spirit'" (John 1:32, 33).

The Father "baptized" Jesus in His Spirit. In turn, Jesus takes of the Father's Spirit (which is now also His own Spirit) and baptizes His followers with it. Just before Jesus ascended, He told His disciples, " 'You will be baptized with the Holy Spirit not many days from now' " (Acts 1:5). A few days later, at the feast of Pentecost, the sound of a rushing wind filled the house, and tongues of fire separated and rested on each one of them, "and they were all filled with the Holy Spirit" (Acts 2:4). Peter explained to all who were listening that the gift of the Holy Spirit was also available to whoever would repent and be baptized in the name of Jesus (Acts 2:38).

When a researcher wants to develop a new variety of tree that has better-tasting fruit, is more productive, or is more disease resistant, he conducts a large breeding program until finally a tree with the desirable characteristics emerges. Then the researcher takes branches from that one good tree and grafts them onto other root stock. The first tree came about because the researcher engaged in a transformative process. In turn, that one tree becomes the source for transformation to thousands or millions of other trees. That is how it is with Jesus. The Father gave Jesus His Spirit, and Jesus in turn gives His transforming Spirit to those who follow Him.

A fourth aspect in which Jesus' intimacy with the Father is a model for us is His status. He is the Son of the Father. You recall that when Jesus healed a person on the Sabbath, the Jews confronted Him about it. He replied, saying, " 'My Father is working until now, and I myself am working' " (John 5:17). The Jews became even more determined to kill Him, "because

He not only was breaking the Sabbath, but also was calling God His own Father, making Himself equal with God" (verse 18). We see here that Jesus claimed to be the Son of the Father.

While Jesus is God, He clarified that He is not equal to the Father in authority but is submissive to the Father in every respect. Jesus told them,

> "Truly, truly, I say to you, the Son can do nothing of Himself, unless it is something He sees the Father doing; for whatever the Father does, these things the Son also does in like manner. For the Father loves the Son, and shows Him all things that He Himself is doing; and the Father will show Him greater works than these, so that you will marvel" (verses 19, 20).

Jesus is the Son of the Father; in like manner He has made a way for us to be sons of the Father.

After Jesus arose from the tomb, He appeared to Mary. They enjoyed a beautiful reunion, and then He said to her, " 'Stop clinging to Me, for I have not yet ascended to the Father; but go to My brethren and say to them, "I ascend to My Father and your Father, and My God and your God" ' " (John 20:17). Jesus puts our relationship to the Father in the same light as His relationship to the Father.

Suppose a man owns a store, and he hires a manager to run it. The manager then hires a cashier and someone to stock the shelves. The relationship of all three of these workers to the owner is that of employees. In a similar way, when we enter into oneness with Jesus, we then relate to the Father as our Father.

The intimacy that Jesus has with the Father is a model for the intimacy He wants us to have with Himself. This intimacy includes the love He and the Father have for one another, the name they share, the Holy Spirit whom the Father gave to Jesus, and Jesus' status related to the Father.

Jesus Is Our Example in the Works His Father Gave Him to Do

The second main area where Jesus' unity with the Father is a model for us is in the works that the Father gave Him to do. If you think of Jesus' mission, what are some words you would use to describe it? He came to save the lost, to show us the Father, to teach us the ways of God. These things are, in turn, what He wants us to do. After Jesus rose from the dead, He came to the apostles, revealed Himself to them, and said, "'Peace be with you; as the Father has sent Me, I also send you'" (John 20:21). The commission that the Father gave to Jesus was the commission He, in turn, gave to His disciples. We are to seek and save the lost. We are to reveal Jesus just as He revealed the Father. We are to serve as He served. We are to be what He was.

I work at a medical device manufacturer, and the company has a mission statement. Shortly after I was employed, I received a little bronze medallion with the primary tenet of the mission embossed on the face of it. It sits on my desk at work. This is not just the mission of the CEO. It is not just the mission of the executive officers. Rather, it is the mission of every one of the employees. In a similar manner, when we are united with Christ, the mission of the Father that He gave to the Son is also your mission and my mission.

Part of that mission is to love others. We are to love as Jesus loved us. John wrote,

> By this the love of God was manifested in us, that God has sent His only begotten Son into the world so that we might live through Him. In this is love, not that we loved God, but that He loved us and sent His Son to be the propitiation for our sins. Beloved, if God so loved us, we also ought to love one another (1 John 4:9–11).

My family and I recently flew to the west coast for a vacation. We encountered travel delays on the return trip and ended up flying into Salt Lake City around midnight. Our connecting flight was at 5:50 a.m., so there was not enough time to get a hotel. We decided to make the best of it by resting in the airport. I scouted around to find where there might be a good spot, and Amy and the kids settled down to wait. When I returned, Amy had a surprised smile on her face. Apparently, four gate agents passing by saw her sitting with four young kids, and they took pity on her. One of the gate agents brought a whole bag of water bottles, and another found a bench that could be used as a bed. A third called the facilities at the airport and requested cots. When all was said and done, we had an unexpectedly restful night compared to what we were anticipating. Those gate agents looked for the need and met it.

That kind of attitude we should have with one another. Day by day, we should strive to practice looking for the need and meeting it. I will be the first to admit I am not very good at it, but I am trying. Little by little I am learning, and I will press on to do even better in the future. That is what God wants us to do. We should "do good to all people, and especially to those who are of the household of the faith" (Galatians 6:10).

A second aspect of the works of the Father that Jesus wants us to emulate is His obedience to the Father. He said, " 'I have come down from heaven, not to do My own will, but the will of Him who sent Me' " (John 6:38). Then He described how we, too, are to carry out His teachings just as Jesus did the will of the Father. He said, " 'Unless you eat the flesh of the Son of Man and drink His blood, you have no life in yourselves' " (verse 53). He went on to say, " 'As the living Father sent Me, and I live because of the Father, so he who eats Me, he also will live because of Me' " (verse 57). He was not talking about the physical part of Himself, as we have studied already, but He was talking about His Spirit that is contained in His words.

He stated very clearly, " 'It is the Spirit who gives life; the flesh profits nothing; the words that I have spoken to you are spirit and are life' " (verse 63). Jesus wants us to have His teachings in our hearts just as He had the teachings of the Father in His heart. He did the will of the Father. The way Jesus carried out the will of the Father is a perfect example of the way Jesus wants us to carry out His teachings in our own lives.

A third aspect in which Jesus' works are a model for us is His forgiveness of sins. Some people once brought a paralyzed man to Jesus, and He told the man, " 'Son, your sins are forgiven' " (Mark 2:5). Some of the people questioned His right to forgive sins, but Jesus said,

> "Which is easier, to say to the paralytic, 'Your sins are forgiven'; or to say, 'Get up, and pick up your pallet and walk'? But so that you may know that the Son of Man has authority on earth to forgive sins"—He said to the paralytic, "I say to you, get up, pick up your pallet and go home" (verses 9–11).

The man did just as Jesus said, and the people were amazed. In this story we see that Jesus had authority to forgive sins. The Father had given this authority to Jesus (John 5:22).

Jesus gave similar authority to His followers when He commissioned them to spread the gospel. Into their hands He placed the responsibility of calling people to repentance. He said to them, " 'Receive the Holy Spirit. If you forgive the sins of any, their sins have been forgiven them; if you retain the sins of any, they have been retained' " (John 20:22, 23). If His disciples, and thereby the church, preached the pure gospel and the hearers repented, they would be forgiven their sins through the blood of Jesus. If the hearers did not acknowledge their sin, they would not be forgiven. The disciples would have discharged their responsibility by offering the words of salvation, and forgiveness would come to those to whom they imparted them. If Jesus' followers kept those words to themselves, people would die in their sins for lack of the words of Christ. In this sense the followers of Jesus have authority to forgive sins. Christ had authority from the Father to forgive sins, and Christ's followers share in that authority to forgive by revealing the teachings of Christ.

A fourth aspect of His works is love for one another. We already read Jesus' statement that " 'just as the Father has loved Me, I have also loved you' " (John 15:9). But Jesus went on to say, " 'This is My commandment, that you love one another, just as I have loved you' " (verse 12). It was so important to Jesus that we love one another that He gave us a positive command to do it. Love is the proof that we have come into a right relationship with God.

When I was a child, I collected rocks. One of the pieces in that collection was a chunk of magnetite. A property of magnetite is that it naturally produces a magnetic field around it. When iron powder is placed on it, the powder forms spiky protrusions as the powder aligns itself with the magnetic field produced by the magnetite. Just as a magnetic field is a natural outflow from a piece of magnetite, love is the natural outflow from a life filled with the Spirit of God.

In this section we have seen that Jesus is our example in the works that His Father gave Him to do. Just as the Father gave works to Jesus, Jesus in turn gives works to His followers. Those works include His mission to love others, His commitment to do the will of the Father, His forgiveness of sins, and His love for His brethren. We should emulate Him in all of these aspects.

Jesus Is Our Example in His Suffering for the Father's Sake

The third area where Jesus' relationship with the Father is

a model for the relationship we have with Him is His suffering for the Father's sake. When a person becomes united with Christ, he also shares in Christ's sufferings. Jesus said, " 'If the world hates you, you know that it has hated Me before it hated you. If you were of the world, the world would love its own; but because you are not of the world, but I chose you out of the world, because of this the world hates you' " (John 15:18, 19).

Believers are hated in the world. Why? Because Satan hates Jesus, and when a person becomes united with Christ, that means Satan hates that person just as he hated Christ. We can expect to be treated just as Jesus was treated. Jesus was clear regarding this subject. He did not want us to be surprised. Yes, knowing Jesus is life itself. Yes, He has great things in store for us. Yes, He is more than worth it in the end. But we are going to have a little bit of trouble before that is fully consummated. I say a "little bit" in the sense of a short duration, but the trouble is severe, just as it was severe for Jesus. History bears record of those who have suffered for their faithfulness to Christ. Millions have been imprisoned, burned at the stake, and beheaded because of their love for Christ. Even today the news recounts tales of persecution that rages on in certain countries.

Jesus wants us to be aware of the things we may have to endure so that when they come, we are not taken by surprise. Peter wrote,

> Beloved, do not be surprised at the fiery ordeal among you, which comes upon you for your testing, as though some strange thing were happening to you; but to the degree that you share the sufferings of Christ, keep on rejoicing, so that also at the revelation of His glory you may rejoice with exultation. If you are reviled for the name of Christ, you are blessed, because the Spirit of glory and of God rests on you (1 Peter 4:12–14).

The very persecutions that seem hard to endure provide evidence that we are united with God.

In the last chapter we studied how, in Jesus' defense of His claim to be the Son of God, He revealed the level of unity that you and I can have with God. But there is more to the story. Jesus quoted from Psalm 82 when He said, " 'Has it not been written in your Law, "I said, 'You are gods?' " ' " (John 10:34). Psalm 82 opens with a description of God presiding over an assembly and rendering judgment among the gods. It conveys the sense that these "gods" are gathered around to hear the judgments of God and follow them. The verse Jesus quoted states, "I said, 'You are gods, and all of you are sons of the Most High' " (Psalm 82:6). These gods that hang on God's every word are more descriptively called "sons of the Most High"— the ones about whom John wrote when He said, "As many as received Him, to them He gave the right to become children of God, even to those who believe in His name" (John 1:12). Note that just a few verses earlier, John clarified that His name is "the Word." The ones who receive Him in the form of His words are called "children of God."

The psalm's very next verse carries a clear notice that not all will be smooth sailing for these "sons of the Most High." The passage states, "Nevertheless you will die like men and fall like any one of the princes" (Psalm 82:6, 7). In fact, most of the psalm describes a climate of persecution. At the very heart of one of the passages that most explicitly declares the believers' relationship to God is a description of oppression. When we become united with God, we are liable to encounter suffering, sorrow, and even death. "All who desire to live godly in Christ Jesus will be persecuted" (2 Timothy 3:12). But if we are faithful and endure to the end, He will more than make it worth any trouble we may undergo in this brief lifetime. He will give us the crown of life, fellowship with Him throughout all eternity, and a share in His immeasurable glory.

My grandfather was a tax assessor. Many people viewed him much like an IRS agent. He would go around and assess the value of various properties, and if the value of a property had increased, then that person's taxes would increase. When people saw him coming, they were not always pleased. One day he pulled into a certain man's driveway. The man saw him coming, grabbed his shotgun, and began firing over my grandfather's car into the trees behind him. My grandfather said he put his car in reverse and sped out of there so fast that you would wonder how he even kept the car under control.

Now suppose my grandfather got back to the office and said to his assistant, "Hey, that guy just shot at me. Maybe you will have better luck." And suppose my grandfather sent his assistant to the man's house to conduct the assessment in his stead. Do you think it would go any better for his assistant? Not at all. The assistant would receive the same treatment as my grandfather received, because both of them had the same purpose. When we become united with God, it is similar—the way Jesus was treated is the way you and I can expect to be treated by those who do not love God. The persecution Jesus endured for the Father's sake is a model of the persecution you and I may encounter for His sake.

Jesus Is Our Example in His Resurrection by the Father's Power

The fourth area where Jesus' relationship with the Father is a model for us is in His resurrection. Paul wrote,

If Christ is in you, though the body is dead because of sin, yet the spirit is alive because of righteousness. But if the Spirit of Him who raised Jesus from the dead dwells in you, He who raised Christ Jesus from the dead will also give life to your mortal bodies through His Spirit who dwells in you (Romans 8:10, 11).

Jesus was raised because of the Father's Spirit in Him. In like manner, believers are raised because of Jesus' Spirit dwelling in them, and Jesus' Spirit is ultimately the Father's Spirit.

One aspect of this point is especially intriguing. According to the Bible, who alone is immortal? Paul explicitly says that it is God "who alone possesses immortality" (1 Timothy 6:16). Do angels possess immortality? No. Some angels may live forever, but that does not mean they have conquered the capacity to die. Satan is an angel, but he is going to be destroyed. (See Ezekiel 28:14, 18, 19.) Therefore it is clear that angels do not naturally possess immortality. But then Paul spoke of the resurrection and how it will happen

> in a moment, in the twinkling of an eye, at the last trumpet; for the trumpet will sound, and the dead will be raised imperishable, and we will be changed. For this perishable must put on the imperishable, and this mortal must put on immortality. But when this perishable will have put on the imperishable, and this mortal will have put on immortality, then will come about the saying that is written, "Death is swallowed up in victory" (1 Corinthians 15:52–54).

Did you catch the implication? God alone possesses immortality, but at the resurrection He will grant immortality to all believers. The immortality that Jesus had through the Father, He passes on to you and to me if we are faithful and we love Him to the end. Here is yet another evidence of the marvelous oneness He is bringing about between Himself and those who follow Him.

Jesus Is Our Example in the Glory Given Him by the Father

The fifth area where the relationship Jesus had with the Father is a model for the relationship He wants us to have with

Him is in the glory He experienced from the Father. Jesus promised rewards to those who will follow Him, saying,

"He who overcomes, and he who keeps My deeds until the end, to him I will give authority over the nations; and he shall rule them with a rod of iron, as the vessels of the potter are broken to pieces, as I also have received authority from My Father" (Revelation 2:26, 27).

Some of the authority Jesus received from the Father, He in turn intends to share with those who are faithful to Him. A part of the kingdom He is establishing includes His followers not only being subjects of the kingdom but His making them into kings in that kingdom. He told His apostles, " 'You are those who have stood by Me in My trials; and just as My Father has granted Me a kingdom, I grant you that you may eat and drink at My table in My kingdom, and you will sit on thrones judging the twelve tribes of Israel' " (Luke 22:28–30). So He grants a kingdom to His followers just as He was granted a kingdom by His Father.

Not only does He share His authority, but He shares His very position with His followers. Jesus promised, " 'He who overcomes, I will grant to him to sit down with Me on My throne, as I also overcame and sat down with My Father on His throne' " (Revelation 3:21). When Jesus overcame and sat down with the Father on His throne, the purpose was not just to be in close physical proximity to the Father. The Father gave Him authority over the entire universe. When we overcome, we will sit down on the throne of Jesus, which is the throne of the Father. We will become kings. We will become rulers with Christ. The glory that Jesus received from the Father is a model of the glory that Jesus will give to His followers.

A Picture of Unity

In this chapter we have studied how the relationship Jesus

has with the Father is a model of the relationship Jesus wants us to have with Him. Now that the pieces of the puzzle are out in the open, let's put them together so that a clear picture emerges of what it means to be united with God.

First, the intimacy Jesus had with the Father is the level of intimacy He wants us to have with Him. The love shared between the Father and the Son is the level of love He wants us to have with Him. The name that the Father shared with Jesus is the name He passes on to you and to me. The Holy Spirit Jesus had from the Father is the same Holy Spirit Jesus took and gave to you and to me. The Father conferred on Jesus the status of Son; and when one becomes united with Christ, Jesus confers on that person the same status of son of God. The way Jesus did the works of the Father is the way you and I should carry out the works of the Father. The commission given to Jesus by the Father is the commission Jesus gave to you and to me. The love for others that Jesus demonstrated is the love that you and I should also demonstrate. The obedience Jesus had to the Father is a model of the obedience we should have to Jesus. The Father gave Jesus authority on earth to forgive sins; in like manner Jesus gave His followers authority on earth to bring about forgiveness of sins by sharing His words. The suffering Jesus endured for the Father's sake is the same kind of suffering we will endure for Jesus' sake. The resurrection Jesus experienced through the Father's power is an example of the resurrection we will experience through Jesus' power, which is the Father's power. The glory that the Father gave to Jesus, Jesus will also share with us. The authority Jesus has from the Father to rule the nations with a rod of iron, He will also share with you and me. The kingdom He received from the Father He is passing on to you and to me. The position on the Father's throne He received from the Father, Jesus will share with you and with me. Astonishing! The shocking magnitude of His favor toward all who trust Him leaves me without adequate words to describe it. Look for yourself and contemplate the unequaled love of God—that He would make us one with Him!

This mighty love of God is what awakens a response of love in our hearts. Behind all of these stupendous rewards is someone who spared no expense to lavish His love on you, and He craves for you to love Him in return. When a response of love awakens in our hearts, the motivation goes deeper than the mighty rewards God offers. The glory of these rewards pales in comparison to the loving One who produced them. He and His love are what captivate our attention and spur a mighty motivation in our hearts to give our full allegiance to Him.

When our response is motivated by love, our attitude will be the same attitude that Jesus had. Paul exhorted the people, "Have this attitude in yourselves which was also in Christ Jesus, who, although He existed in the form of God, did not regard equality with God a thing to be grasped" (Philippians 2:5, 6). You and I have the opportunity to become sons of God. But just as Jesus did not pursue equal authority with the Father, we should not pursue equal authority with Jesus. Rather, we should submit ourselves to Him just as He submitted Himself to the Father.

Even the stunning rewards that may first attract our attention are but a mirror reflecting the glory of a deeper experience. These rewards are just the wrapping on the gift. To give a nod of amazed acknowledgement to those rewards is appropriate, but the way to obtain them is to submit ourselves wholeheartedly to God. We adopt the same attitude Jesus displayed. He did not consider equality with God a thing to be grasped,

> but emptied Himself, taking the form of a bond-servant, and being made in the likeness of men. Being found in appearance as a man, He humbled Himself by becoming obedient to the point of death, even death on a cross. For

this reason also, God highly exalted Him, and bestowed on Him the name which is above every name, so that at the name of Jesus every knee will bow, of those who are in heaven and on earth and under the earth, and that every tongue will confess that Jesus Christ is Lord, to the glory of God the Father (verses 7–11).

Jesus humbled Himself, and then the Father highly exalted Him. In like manner, if we humble ourselves as Jesus did, fully surrendering to the heart-melting love of Christ, He will one day exalt us and grant to us a share in His glory. This is a high calling, but let's press on into full surrender to Christ.

Discussion Questions:

1. What are five areas where Jesus' relationship with the Father is an exact model for the believer's relationship with Jesus?

2. What are two dangers related to this subject of unity with God against which we must carefully guard?

3. Describe the level of intimacy God desires to have with you.

4. What does it mean to be called by Jesus' name?

5. Based on the example of Jesus' relationship with the Father, what are some of the works God wants us to do?

6. Based on the description of unity with God found in the Scriptures, list some attributes of God that come to your mind.

7. Give an example of when you have seen someone suffer for their unity with Christ.

8. Compare the unity believers can have with Jesus with the unity believers can have with the Father. How are

they similar? How are they different?

9. Describe the causes for unity with God and the effects of it.

10. Many popular but false theories are related to unity with God. Describe one of them and contrast it with the truth as explained by the Scriptures.

11. Suppose you wanted to let your husband or wife (or some other special person) know that you love them. And suppose you wanted to do it in such a way that it would deeply impress upon them the depth of your affection for them. What would you do? Compare those efforts with what God has done to let you know that He loves you. How are they similar? How are they different?

12. Compare your relationship with Jesus to Jesus' relationship with the Father. What areas need to change in order for you to emulate Jesus' example more perfectly? What is one step you will take today to bring about those changes?

CHAPTER FOUR

Guaranteed Answers to Prayer

J esus gave an amazing promise the night before He was crucified. He said,

"In that day you will not question Me about anything. Truly, truly, I say to you, if you ask the Father for anything in My name, He will give it to you. Until now you have asked for nothing in My name; ask and you will receive, so that your joy may be made full" (John 16:23, 24).

A childhood friend of mine is named Jennifer. She married and had a son, and she and her husband named him Connor. When Connor was thirteen years old, he was diagnosed with leukemia. His parents, of course, got for him the best medical care they could find. Moreover, they earnestly prayed for him, and they enlisted the prayers of their family, friends, and church members as well.

Some months later, to everyone's joy, the leukemia went into remission. Shortly after that time I saw Jennifer's father at a camp meeting, and I asked him how things were going. He said, "Well, things are going fine for me, but Connor is not doing well. The leukemia has returned. The doctors say that there is not much they can do at this point, so his parents are trying some herbal remedies, but it is not looking good. Would you please pray for him?" I said, "Well sure, I would be happy to." So I sent my requests heavenward, as did all of his other family and friends who were praying for him.

About a week later, Jennifer's mother posted this note on Facebook. "Thank you, dear friends, for all of your prayers. Connor died about 6:30 our time this evening. He said before he died that he would meet his family on the sea of glass. He is now resting, awaiting Jesus' coming and the resurrection that will take place at that time. We look forward to that time when we shall see Connor again."

Three Synonyms for Praying in Jesus' Name

Today we are going to look at why sometimes our prayers are not answered, and how it is that Jesus' promise has never failed that if we ask for anything in His name it will be given to us. As the text in John indicates, there is one prerequisite for having guaranteed answers to our prayers. That one prerequisite is that we ask in Jesus' name.

The key point I would like us to take away from this chapter is that asking in Jesus' name means to ask as one with Jesus. That encompasses the idea that we ask in a state of full surrender to Him, and we ask according to His will. This topic was actually a favorite subject of John. At least four times he wrote about how we can have guaranteed answers to our prayers. We read one of those texts already. I would like to look at the other three texts to draw some conclusions as to what it means to pray in Jesus' name. That way, we can find a clearer picture of what Jesus was really trying to say.

The first of the three synonymous texts is John 15:7, where Jesus said, " 'If you abide in Me, and My words abide in you, ask whatever you wish, and it will be done for you.' " Therefore, one conclusion we can draw about praying in Jesus' name is that it happens when we abide in Jesus and have His words abide in us.

The second stop is 1 John 5:14 and 15, where John wrote,

This is the confidence which we have before Him, that, if we ask anything according to His will, He hears us. And if we know that He hears us in whatever we ask, we know that we have the requests which we have asked from Him.

Therefore the second conclusion for praying in Jesus' name is that we ask according to His will.

Our third stop is 1 John 3:22. There it says, "Whatever we ask we receive from Him, because we keep His commandments and do the things that are pleasing in His sight." Clearly, our commandment keeping and doing what pleases Him are an important part of receiving answers from Jesus.

Putting the clues together, here is the picture that emerges. Praying in Jesus' name means that we abide in Jesus and have His words abide in us, that we ask according to His will, and that we keep His commandments and do what is pleasing in His sight.

A State of Being

Praying in Jesus' name is a state of being, not a phrase that we add to the middle or the end of our prayers. Praying in Jesus' name means that we pray as one with Jesus. In the great high priestly prayer that Jesus prayed on the night before He was crucified, He said, " 'I am no longer in the world; and yet they themselves are in the world, and I come to You. Holy Father, keep them in Your name, the name which You have given Me, that they may be one even as We are' " (John 17:11).

If the disciples had to be kept in Jesus' name, then "in Jesus' name" was not a phrase they were to use in their prayers but rather a place they had to be. Praying in Jesus' name is a state of being. In order to pray in Jesus' name, we must be in Jesus' name.

After Jesus had gone back to heaven, Peter and John went to the temple. As they were about to enter, they saw a lame man, who asked them for money. Peter replied, " 'I do not possess silver and gold, but what I do have I give to you: in the name of Jesus Christ the Nazarene—walk!' " (Acts 3:6). Immediately the man jumped to his feet and went with Peter and John into the temple, leaping and running and praising God. When Peter healed the man, he used the phrase *in Jesus' name,* but there was no power in the mere words that he said. The power stemmed from the way Peter lived and the thing that he asked God for. Praying in Jesus' name means that we pray for the right things and we live the right way.

A man named Sceva had seven sons, and they tried the same thing. They attempted to drive out a demon from a possessed man, saying, " 'I adjure you by Jesus whom Paul preaches.' " But the evil spirit, speaking through the possessed man, replied, " 'I recognize Jesus, and I know about Paul, but who are you?' " (Acts 19:13–15). Then he leaped on them and beat them up, and they ran away naked and bleeding. Therefore, just saying the name of Jesus or adding a phrase to our prayers is not what has any effect; rather, the effectiveness of praying in Jesus' name comes from us being in Jesus.

The first few chapters of this book delved deep into the importance of internalizing Jesus' words. When we take in those words, we end up taking in His Spirit, because His Spirit is embodied in those words. By doing so, we become one with Him in a beautiful love relationship. That unity with Him is what Jesus was talking about when He said that if we ask the Father for anything in His name, it will be given to us. In order to have guaranteed answers to our prayers we must be in Jesus' name—in other words, we must live the right way and pray for the right things.

A few years ago, I had my own consulting business. One of my clients got caught up in the economic downturn of 2008, and he eventually went out of business. When his business folded, all of his accounts were turned over to collections agents. One of those agents called me because I had done work for the man, and he demanded that I pay his debts. He said, "If you do not pay, I am going to sue you. The police are going to show up at your door, they are going to serve you papers, you are going to have to go to court, and not only are you going to have to pay all these debts, you are going to have to pay all the court costs on top of it too. Which credit card would you like to use to pay today?"

I said, "Wait a minute! These are not my debts. These are another man's debts." We talked a couple of times on the phone, and it was always the same high-pressure techniques he used to get me to pay the other man's debts.

Finally I said, "If you feel you need to have me pay, you can take it to court, and if the courts decide that I should pay, then I will pay." Interestingly, he never sued me, he never had the police come and serve papers at my door, and, in fact, I never heard from the man again. The reality of the matter was, no matter what he said with his mouth, or how many threats he made, those debts were not my debts—they were somebody else's debts.

When it comes to praying in Jesus' name, it is similar. It does not matter much what we say. Simply uttering the words "in Jesus' name" does not obligate the Father to grant our desires. What matters is the substance behind the words. Are we in Jesus? In other words, are we fully submitted to His authority, and are we praying in accordance with His will?

Jesus Is Our Example in Prayer

Jesus is our example in all points, including prayer. Jesus had power to do the marvelous miracles He did because He prayed in the Father's name. In other words, He prayed as one with the Father, fully under His authority and in accordance with His will. Jesus Himself declared,

> "Truly, truly, I say to you, the Son can do nothing of Himself, unless it is something He sees the Father doing; for whatever the Father does, these things the Son also does in like manner. For the Father loves the Son, and shows Him all things that He Himself is doing; and the Father will show Him greater works than these, so that you will marvel" (John 5:19, 20).

The stunning miracles Jesus performed did not originate within Himself, but the Father showed them to Jesus—He revealed His will to Jesus. Now, make no mistake, all authority in heaven and on earth has been given to Jesus, but that authority was given to Him because He was one with the Father. The Father granted it to Him because He obeyed the Father in everything, and He asked according to the Father's will. Jesus is in complete unity with the Father.

In your mind's eye, envision the crippled man lying beside the pool of Bethesda. Jesus approached him and asked, " 'Do you wish to get well?' " (John 5:6). According to the truth of Jesus' other statement in John 5, when Jesus asked the crippled man this question, in His state of being a Son of the Father, Jesus possessed no more healing power in and of Himself than you or I do. The man replied with a lamentable story about how he had no one to put him into the water when the conditions were right. Jesus finally told him, " 'Get up, pick up your pallet and walk' " (verse 8). Immediately the man became well, picked up his pallet, and began to walk.

Jesus possessed power to heal, but the power was not His own power; it was the Father's power. The Father gave Him this power because it was the Father's will. It was a work that His Father had revealed to Him. Therefore, Jesus possessed the two ingredients for a guaranteed answer to His prayer. First, He lived the right way, and second, He prayed in accordance with the Father's will.

A Passionate Pursuit of God's Will

Just as Jesus prayed in the Father's name, we are to pray in Jesus' name. And the promise is that if we ask anything according to His will, He hears us. Herein is a striking opportunity. If we first wholeheartedly set our hearts to know and do God's will, there is no request too great if we can just figure out what God's will is for sure, and pray according to it. We should therefore passionately, ravenously, search the Scriptures to find what the will of God is, because there is no limit to the blessings we may request that are in line with His will.

It seems we often have an attitude that we can only pray about the things that can be solved by chance, or only make requests before things happen. Nobody can restore sight to one who is born blind, or cure cerebral palsy, or raise someone who has been dead for more than a few minutes, so we tend not to pray about those things. However, God is not limited in any of these situations, for Jesus cured many people with similar conditions when He was here on earth. I fear we limit our prayers to those things that could happen by chance because such prayers require no faith. In other words, such prayers require no repentance, no aligning of ourselves with God's will, no crucifixion of selfish desires. We pray about the weather, we pray for people who have illnesses that are treatable, we pray for material things we want, but resolution to all of these problems can happen naturally. Even a wicked person could pray for these things, and it would look like his prayers at times were answered. Undoubtedly God does answer some prayers in all of these situations, but believers need not limit themselves to prayers that could be solved naturally. Anything, no matter how great, is fair game if they know it is God's will.

True Fasting

God helps us get where we want to go when that destination is where He wants us to go. Prayer is not so much about making our wishes known to God as it is about figuring out what His wishes are for us. Prayer is not so much to convince God to do what we want so much as to align ourselves with His desires.

The prophet Isaiah spoke about having guaranteed answers to our prayers. He introduced the topic by showing the people the inadequacy of their fasts. They were fasting, but they were not aligning their lives with what God wanted. He said, " 'Behold, you fast for contention and strife and to strike with a wicked fist. You do not fast like you do today to make your voice heard on high' " (Isaiah 58:4). So, on the one hand, the people wanted their voice to be heard on high. They wanted God to pay attention to their requests. But they wanted to live their own way.

A friend once confided, "I am struggling to surrender my life to God because I am afraid He does not want me to date my girlfriend. If I give all to God, He might change my desires so that I will not want to pursue this relationship anymore. I just do not know if I am ready to take that chance." Whether it was God's will for him to let that relationship go, I do not know. But the reality was that my friend was trying to hang on to his desires and follow God at the same time. That is the attitude of the people that Isaiah rebuked.

In Isaiah 58:5 God speaks about fasting again. " 'Is it a fast like this which I choose, a day for a man to humble himself? Is it for bowing one's head like a reed and for spreading out sackcloth and ashes as a bed? Will you call this a fast, even an acceptable day to the LORD?' " In effect, God is saying, "The way you are pursuing Me in this manner is not acceptable to Me. This type of humbling of yourselves is not pleasing to Me.

Rather, your obedient spirit is what I want." He went on in Isaiah, saying,

Is this not the fast which I choose, to loosen the bonds of wickedness, to undo the bands of the yoke, and to let the oppressed go free and break every yoke? Is it not to divide your bread with the hungry and bring the homeless poor into the house; when you see the naked, to cover him; and not to hide yourself from your own flesh? Then your light will break out like the dawn, and your recovery will speedily spring forth; and your righteousness will go before you; the glory of the Lord will be your rear guard. Then you will call, and the LORD will answer; you will cry, and He will say, 'Here I am' " (verses 6–9).

It is a wonderful chapter that contains much about what God really wants from us.

Delight Yourself in the Lord

King David wrote, "Delight yourself in the LORD; and He will give you the desires of your heart" (Psalm 37:4). If we delight ourselves in the Lord, our desires will be for Him.

Suppose a woman wants a million dollars, and she prays, "God, please give me a million dollars." When she does not get what she requested, she thinks, "Well, maybe it is because I have sin in my life." So she repents and tries to follow what God says through Isaiah, because she wants that million dollars. Then she prays again, "God, please give me a million dollars." Do you see what is wrong with that situation? Rather than turning from her desires and turning to God's desires, her ultimate goal is still the million dollars. She is attempting to manipulate God into giving her what she wants. Isaiah is indicating that she should turn away from her desire and earnestly pursue what God desires. Then she can pray according to God's will and receive guaranteed answers to her prayers.

Often at prayer meetings people request prayer for health or their finances or better jobs. They base their prayers primarily on what they want rather than what God wants. What God is saying through Isaiah is that we need to align ourselves with what God wants, and then we will have guaranteed answers to our prayers.

Imagine a prayer meeting where a woman raises her hand and says, "Please pray for me that I may loosen the bonds of wickedness." And a man adds, "Please pray for me so that I can divide my bread with the hungry." And a child interjects, "Please pray for me that I may know how to clothe those who are struggling to provide for themselves." Wow, what a prayer meeting that would be! As Isaiah said, "Then your light will break out like the dawn and your recovery will speedily spring forth."

The Blue Ridge Parkway is a scenic drive that winds through the tops of the Appalachian mountains. In 2004 the remnants of Hurricane Frances blew over the mountains of North Carolina and dropped twelve to eighteen inches of rain. Numerous landslides swept down from the mountains, including one that carried a section of the Blue Ridge Parkway hundreds of feet down the hillside. The National Park Service closed an eight-mile section of the road in order to prevent accidents. Sometime later we went driving on the Blue Ridge Parkway nearby. My hope was that they had fixed the road and reopened the closed stretch, but to my disappointment we rounded a corner and there was a gate across the road and signs saying that the area was still closed. Nothing could be done but to turn around and leave.

Suppose that, rather than leaving, we had parked by the gate until somebody else came along. And imagine that we had motioned to them and called out, "Hey, come over here and give us a hand. This gate is blocking our progress. Will you help us break that lock and open the gate so we can go on up the mountain?" Do you think those people would provide any assistance? They would emphatically say, "No, we are not helping you! The road is out up ahead. You might have an accident, and not only you, but anyone coming behind you would be at risk too." We in our human wisdom can see that it would be not wise to help somebody go on to encounter such a hazard. And it is the same with God. He does not help us go in a direction that will be detrimental for His kingdom. But He will help us go in a direction that is beneficial to His kingdom. In short, if our deepest desire is to find His will and conform our lives to it, then He will help us get where we desire to go.

Two Classes of Prayer

Two classes of acceptable prayers are available to us. The first is prayers we know for sure are according to the will of God. Those are prayers for which we are guaranteed to have an answer. The second class is prayers for when we have uncertainty about what the will of God is. To pray about all those things is not wrong. I do not want anybody to finish reading this chapter and think, "Well, I can only pray for what I know for sure is God's will." True, we should seek out the will of God and pray according to it, but by no means should we limit ourselves just to the things that we know for sure are His will. Jesus did not limit Himself just to the things that He knew for sure were the Father's will. In the Garden of Gethsemane He prayed, " 'My Father, if it is possible, let this cup pass from Me; yet not as I will, but as You will' " (Matthew 26:39). He was saying, in effect, "If there is some opportunity other than Me dying, please, let's follow that course instead. Yet, if there is not that opportunity, do not follow what I want but what You want." That is a safe prayer for us too. We can pray in the same way and take all of our requests to God. Peter wrote, "Cast all your anxiety on him because he cares for you" (1 Peter 5:7, NIV). Let's not limit ourselves. Let's cast all our cares on Him. "Be anxious for nothing, but in everything by prayer and supplication with thanksgiving let your requests be made known to God" (Philippians 4:6). Yet at the same time, it will make our prayers more efficient if we will seek out the will of God and pray according to it.

One day our family visited a picnic area on the shore of a lake. Our toddler Matthew was running along and tripped, and he scraped his knee when he fell. He wailed loudly for quite some time. Though only a minor scrape, it was bleeding a little bit, so we took him up to the van, washed it, and put a bandage on it. Then we comforted him. If we as earthly human parents care tenderly about the very small things like that in our children's lives, how much more does our Father in heaven care about the things that are going on in our lives? Therefore, let's make our requests known to Him. Let's not limit our prayers just to the things we know for sure are His will. Let's cast our cares on Him, for He cares for us.

A Strong Faith

When we know for sure that something is God's will, we should pray for it, believing that God will give it to us. For example, suppose you see a fellow believer wearing raggedy clothes, and it is evident that he does not have enough money to provide for himself. And suppose you remember the passage in Isaiah 58 about clothing the naked, and you pray to God, "Please, help me clothe that person." You know for sure you are praying according to the will of God because you are praying according to a clear passage of Scripture. When you set about to clothe that person, you must believe that God will enable you. When we have clear direction from the Bible to back up our requests, we should be careful to avoid doubting that God will help.

In Luke 18 Jesus tells the people a parable instructing them that at all times they ought to pray and not lose heart. He said that in a certain village was a judge who did not fear God and did not respect men. A widow came to him pouring out her request to him, and she kept nagging him again and again. He finally said to himself, " 'Even though I do not fear God nor respect man, yet because this widow bothers me, I will give her legal protection, otherwise by continually coming she will wear me out' " (Luke 18:4, 5). Notice that the unrighteous judge helped her because she kept begging for it. How much more will our heavenly Father help those who beg Him for assistance in carrying out what they know for sure is His will?

On Mount Carmel, Elijah prayed that God would send rain on the earth, even though a drought had parched the land for three and a half years. He then sent his servant to see if any rainclouds were forming. The servant returned and told him there was nothing. But God had told Elijah, " 'Go, show yourself to Ahab, and I will send rain on the face of the earth' " (1 Kings 18:1). Therefore Elijah had confidence that he was praying according to the will of God. He bowed again, determined to pray until his request was granted. Time and again the servant returned with the discouraging message that no clouds were forming. Finally, after the seventh trip the servant said, " 'A cloud as small as a man's hand is coming up from the sea' " (verse 44). Sure enough, rain soon pounded the landscape. When we know God's will, we should keep pressing our requests without wavering in our confidence.

A Third Class of Prayer

A third class of prayers exists, but they are ones we want to avoid at all costs. We must be careful not to pray for things that we know for sure are against God's will. God just might give it to us even though He knows it will be bad for us. Though God was the king of Israel, the people requested that they be given a human king to rule them. The prophet Samuel conveyed to them a message from God, warning them of the terrible consequences of this course. He pleaded with them not to reject God as their king, but the people refused to listen to him and kept pressing their request. God consented to their request due to the hardness of their hearts, even though he knew it was not the best course. He gave them King Saul to rule them. Saul started out well but soon turned from the Lord, leading the people to sin against God. The sad outcome could have been prevented if the people had submitted to the clear revelation of God's will rather than continuing to pray in opposition to it.

What Is God's Will?

If it is so important to follow God's will, what then is His will? The answer to that question is so large that it will take a lifetime to study it out. At the same time, we can discern some of God's will very readily. Whatever He commands us, that is obviously His will. A good place to start is the Ten Commandments. Another great source is the teachings of Jesus recorded in the Gospels.

David prophesied of Jesus, saying, "I delight to do Your will, O my God; Your law is within my heart" (Psalm 40:8). God's will is that we carry out His law. That was Jesus' way of operation; that should be our way of operation as well. Doing the will of God and keeping His law—these are tied together. God's commands are some of the clearest statements of His will. They are not just external commands but principles we should apply across broad swaths of our character.

When I think back over my life and the times when I know for sure that my prayers were answered, all the ones I can think of were in relation to keeping God's commandments and keeping His will. Many times when I was tempted, I prayed, "God, I don't have it in me to do what is right, but you can help me. Please, work in me through the power of the Holy Spirit to help me follow you in every area of my life." Out of those times of fervent prayer and tenacious hanging on, beautiful answers to prayer have come.

God's Will May Be More Limited than We Assume

I think many times people are disappointed in their prayer lives because they assume they know what God's will is, when His revealed will is more limited than many think. Here is a little quiz to test your understanding of this concept.

Question 1: According to the Bible, is it God's will to cure a person's disabling disease?

Answer: Maybe. Jesus did heal a lot of people, and ultimately in heaven He will take away all of our bodily diseases and restore perfect health to the redeemed. But in this life there is no guarantee that God will heal us of our disabling diseases. Remember Paul? He had a bodily affliction, and he prayed three times that God would take it away from him, but God declined. Instead He told Paul, " 'My grace is sufficient for you, for My strength is made perfect in weakness' " (2 Corinthians 12:9, NKJV). If we have such a condition, we should still pray about it. If my child comes down with a disease, I am going to pray for him. But this falls into that second class of prayers where we do not know for sure whether it is God's will to heal right then or later. To be clear, when we become one with God, He feels our pain just as though it were happening to Him. He does not take pleasure in allowing us to go through painful circumstances, but sometimes He must act, even when we cannot understand the reasons.

When I was a toddler, my parents took me to the hospital for a procedure to open up one of my tear ducts. Terror welled up inside me when my parents left me, and three or four medical professionals surrounded my bed as they prepared to do the procedure. When I awoke, I was angry with my parents.

Why had they brought me to the hospital to experience this pain? Why had they disappeared when I needed them? Why had they allowed the scary people with the masks and cold instruments to get near me? Finally my dad went to the hospital gift shop and got a little stuffed dog with droopy ears and a sad expression on its face. He gave him to me as an expression of his love and understanding, even though the reasons for his decisions were too difficult to explain. In a similar way, God does not take pleasure in our pain, even if it is His will to lead us through painful circumstances.

Question 2: According to the Bible, is it God's will to protect your children from dying in an accident?

Answer: Maybe. God certainly saved somebody's children when Jesus rescued the disciples out on the Sea of Galilee. They were going to drown, but He calmed the storm. What about Job's children? God allowed Satan to bring a whirlwind, probably a tornado, and it knocked down the place where they were staying. All twelve of them died. Here is what we know for sure is God's will. Jesus said,

> "This is the will of Him who sent Me, that of all He has given Me I lose nothing, but raise it up on the last day. For this is the will of My Father, that everyone who beholds the Son and believes in Him will have eternal life, and I myself will raise him up on the last day" (John 6:39, 40).

Question 3: According to the Bible, is it God's will to prevent you from losing everything you own in a war?

Answer: Maybe. God protected the Israelites when an army of a million Ethiopians came against them. But again, remember Job. He lost all of his camels, oxen, and donkeys to enemy invaders in one day. God's will in this area is unclear, but Jesus did reveal something of God's will related to this topic. He said, " 'Do not store up for yourselves treasures on earth, where moth and rust destroy, and where thieves break in and steal. But store up for yourselves treasures in heaven, where neither moth nor rust destroys, and where thieves do not break in and steal' " (Matthew 6:19, 20).

Question 4: According to the Bible, is it God's will that you sacrifice your own interests in order to care for your aging parents?

Answer: Yes. The fifth commandment says, "Honor your father and your mother, that your days may be prolonged in the land which the LORD your God gives you" (Exodus 20:12). God's commands are His will. If we pray for help in overcoming our natural reluctance to laying down our own interests in order to help our parents, we are guaranteed to have an answer for that request. He will strengthen us to fully comply with His desires.

Question 5: According to the Bible, is it God's will that you be sanctified and that you be cleansed from sin and enabled to love as God loves?

Answer: Yes. The Bible says, "This is the will of God, your sanctification" (1 Thessalonians 4:3). "Sanctify them in the truth; Your word is truth" (John 17:17). "Pursue peace with all men, and the sanctification without which no one will see the Lord" (Hebrews 12:14). Our sanctification is definitely God's will. We can pray for it and be guaranteed to have an answer to our prayers.

Question 6: According to the Bible, is it God's will to help you win the lottery?

Answer: No. One time I asked somebody that question and he quickly responded, "Yes!" Thankfully there was a lot of jest in his tone of voice. Just a few miles from our house are numerous casinos in Tunica, Mississippi. I imagine that millions of prayers have ascended from them, people praying that God will help them win big, but God has not answered even one of those prayers. If those people won, it was just due to chance, not because God intervened. God explicitly said, "You shall not covet" (Exodus 20:17). Paul clearly laid out the will of God when he wrote,

> But those who want to get rich fall into temptation and a snare and many foolish and harmful desires which plunge men into ruin and destruction. For the love of money is a root of all sorts of evil, and some by longing for it have wandered away from the faith and pierced themselves with many griefs (1 Timothy 6:9, 10).

God does not want us to set our hearts on money. If money happens to find us, great. But we should not go seeking for it as though it would provide meaning in our lives. We should be content with just enough money to provide the basic necessities of life. If we find ourselves in possession of more money, then we should use it to build up the kingdom of God.

A Two-Part Challenge

In closing, I want to reemphasize that praying in Jesus' name is much more than just a phrase that we add to our prayers. Rather, it is a way of life. Praying in Jesus' name means to pray as one with Jesus. Praying in Jesus' name means we live the right way and we pray for the right things.

I would like to extend a challenge to you. It is a challenge to search, and to search in two aspects. First, search your heart to see if there is any part of your life where you are not following what you know to be right. Once you have answered that question and have set your heart fully to know and do God's will because of your love for Him, then, second, search for God's will.

If we can determine what God's will is and pray according to it, then there is no request, no matter how great, that will be withheld from us, because He has promised that whatever we ask in His name He will give to us. Let's pray as Jesus in-

structed so that we may ask and receive, that our joy may be
made full.

A Model Prayer

The Lord's Prayer is a wonderful model for those seeking
to pray according to God's will. It presents a perfect summa-
tion of all the elements of oneness with God. It teaches us
how God wants us to pray, and it is a prayer to which we are
guaranteed to have answers because it is in accordance with
God's will. I leave you with this prayer, expanded somewhat
to include the intent I believe Jesus was trying to convey. This
is my prayer for you, and for me, and I hope you will make it
your prayer as well.

"Our Father who is in heaven, You are not just someone
else's Father, but You are our very own Father. Hallowed be
Your name—the name that is so much more than a title,
the name that we can enter into and be called by when we
become one with You. Your kingdom come. You are a king,
and the subjects of Your kingdom must be subject to You,
its king. Your will be done on earth, in our lives, as readily as Your angels do it in heaven. Give us today our daily
bread, the true bread out of heaven. That bread is every
word that proceeds from Your mouth. We deeply hunger
for and long to internalize those words in our lives and act
on them. Forgive us our debts as we also forgive our debt-
ors. Let Your loving and gracious character be replicated
in our lives. Lead us not into temptation, but deliver us
from evil. We zealously desire to distance ourselves from
any action that even hints of evil. For Yours is the kingdom
forever, the kingdom made up of followers who are one
with You. Yours is the power forever, the power because
You rule over us through all ages to come. And Yours is the
glory forever, glory as Your followers worship and adore
You through the ceaseless years of eternity. Amen."

Discussion Questions:

1. What are three synonyms for praying in Jesus' name?

2. What are two classes of acceptable prayers, and one class of dangerous prayers?

3. Summarize in your own words what it means to pray in Jesus' name.

4. Describe the key element of the sort of fast that is pleasing to God.

5. Create a list of things people commonly pray for in which God's will is uncertain.

6. Compose a prayer with at least five requests, all of which are things that you know for certain are God's will. Discuss the evidence upon which you base your conclusions regarding God's will.

7. Think about the last prayer time you had, or the last prayer meeting you attended. What did you pray for? What proportion of those things did you know for sure were God's will? Are you comfortable with the balance, or do you need to add in more things that you know are His will?

8. Analyze some of the prayers of Jesus. Which ones were prayed with full assurance of God's will? How did Jesus know for certain what the will of His Father was? Which prayers were prayed with uncertainty of God's will? See, for example, Matthew 6:9–13; Matthew 11:25, 26; Matthew 26:39–42; Matthew 26:53, 54; Luke 23:34; Luke 23:46; John 11:41, 42; John 12:27, 28; John 17.

9. In five to ten sentences, explain one reason our prayers are sometimes not answered. Avoid repeating the same response as another member in the group.

10. The first chapter in this book asked you to discuss what it really means to believe, and the second chapter asked you to study the unity that God desires to have with us. The present chapter asks you to study what it means to pray in Jesus' name. In what ways are these three topics related, and how does the reading and study you conducted on the former topics inform, enrich, or otherwise affect your understanding of the latter topic?

11. What measures can you take that would foster a church atmosphere centered on finding the will of God and praying according to it? Your first response should outline the measures you would take in fulfilling this task. Your second response should evaluate the pros and cons of the measures proposed by another member in the discussion group.

12. For each of the following prayers, judge which ones are according to the will of God, which ones have uncertainty, and which ones are against God's will. Discuss your reasons.

▶ "God bless America."

▶ "Please help my uncle overcome lung cancer."

▶ "Please give me patience to treat my children kindly, even when they are acting unkindly."

▶ "Please help the Dallas Cowboys win."

▶ "Please bless the food."

▶ "I choose to follow You. Please give me the strength to avoid pornographic websites."

▶ "Sorry about lying. Please help me not get caught, just this once."

▶ "Please help me adjust my schedule so that You are my number one priority."

▶ "Please help us rest well."

▶ "Please guide the Bible study with my neighbors so that I can clearly articulate Your love to them."

▶ "Please help us cook the meth safely."

▶ "Please protect us while we travel."

▶ "Please guide my words as I speak so that it will not be me speaking out of my own human wisdom, but that it will be Your Spirit speaking through me."

CHAPTER FIVE

The Least of These

December 20, 1943, Charles Brown was on his first combat mission, flying a B-17 bomber over Germany. His plane was damaged by flak and badly shot up by German fighter planes. One of his engines was dead, and another one was operating erratically. He was not able to keep up with the rest of his squadron and was left alone in the skies over Germany. As he was nursing his plane along, something caught his attention. He glanced out the window and saw, just three feet off his wingtip, a German Messerschmitt fighter. The co-pilot cried out, "This is a nightmare!"

Charles Brown agreed. "He's going to destroy us."

The pilot of that fighter plane, Franz Stigler, was no ordinary pilot. He was what was known as a flying ace, a pilot who had shot down at least five enemy aircraft. If he shot down one more plane, he would be awarded the Knight's Cross, Germany's highest medal for valor. Furthermore, his only brother had been killed earlier in the war. He had every reason to shoot the B-17 down.

When Franz had seen the B-17 fly over, he jumped in his plane and started after it. As he approached, he expected to receive fire from the plane, but nothing happened. His curiosity was aroused, so he came in a little closer. He saw that the plane's tail was almost entirely gone, and the tail gunner was dead. Large sections of sheet metal were missing. He could even look inside the plane and see crew members attending to the wounded. He felt that to shoot the plane down in that condition would be to violate an internal code, "to fight with fearlessness and restraint, to celebrate victories not death."

Franz eased his plane up beside the cockpit. When he locked eyes with Charles Brown, he saw the look of shock and horror in the pilot's eyes. He also felt that to leave him would be the same as shooting him down, because just a few miles ahead were flak batteries lining the German coast. The disabled plane would not stand a chance of escape. Instead, Franz escorted the B-17 out of German airspace and out over the North Sea. He caught Charles Brown's attention again, saluted him, and banked away, saying to himself, "Good luck, you're in God's hands."

This experience haunted Charles Brown, and decades later he began having nightmares about the flight. Finally, at the suggestion of a friend, he decided to find out what had happened to that pilot. He contacted the editor of a newsletter for German pilots from World War II. The editor agreed to include in one of the issues a quarter-page letter from Charles describing some of the details of the story. In the letter, he asked anybody who knew anything about the pilot to contact him.

To his delight, a few months later, he received a letter in the mail from Franz Stigler himself. Franz had immigrated to Canada and settled in Vancouver. This introduction began a very deep friendship between the two men. They went fishing together, they called each other often on the phone, and they traveled the United States together, sharing their story of what had happened many decades before.

Franz wrote a note inside the cover of a book about airplanes that he gave to Charles Brown. It said, "In 1940, I lost my only brother as a night fighter. On the 20th of December, four days before Christmas, I had the chance to save a B-17 from her destruction, a plane so badly damaged it was a wonder she was still flying. The pilot, Charlie Brown, is for me as precious as my brother was. Thanks Charlie. Your brother, Franz."

Charles Brown and his air force veterans group invited Franz to attend one of their reunions. There, Charles surprised Franz by introducing him to two of the crew members who had been on the plane that Franz spared. The four of them embraced, tears of gratitude flowing down their faces. After a few minutes, they were joined in the emotional embrace by others, including the sons, daughters, and grandchildren of the surviving crew members. These descendants all owed their lives to Franz for the act of mercy he showed to the men on the crippled B-17 many decades earlier.[5]

The way Franz treated those men that day in the skies over Germany was also how he treated their children and their grandchildren, because it could be said that at that time, those children and grandchildren were part of those men. In a similar way, Christ considers those who have His Spirit in them as part of himself, and just as Franz's act of mercy was not just for those men but also an act of mercy to their children and grandchildren, so Christ considers any acts done to those who have His Spirit within them as done to Himself.

How You Treat Christ's Body Is How You Treat Christ

In the first few chapters we studied how, when we take in the words of Christ and make those teachings part of us, the

---

5. Adapted from Adam Makos with Larry Alexander, *A Higher Call* (New York: Berkley Caliber, 2012).

Holy Spirit comes in with that teaching and then Christ considers us as part of Himself. Ultimately, because He is one with the Father, that union makes us one with the Father as well. In this chapter, let's pull back the curtain on the mystery a little further and look at the profound impact this has on our relationships with fellow believers. If the Holy Spirit is within you, then the way that I treat you is the way that I treat Christ. Moreover, if the Holy Spirit is within you and the Holy Spirit is within me, then the way I treat you is the way I treat myself.

Christ's Brothers

Jesus spoke about the day when He would judge the earth, and He said there will be a separation of the people—those who treated Him well separated from those who neglected Him. He will say to the favored ones, " ' "Come, you who are blessed of My Father, inherit the kingdom prepared for you from the foundation of the world. For I was hungry, and you gave Me something to eat; I was thirsty, and you gave Me something to drink; I was a stranger, and you invited Me in; naked, and you clothed Me; I was sick, and you visited Me; I was in prison, and you came to Me" ' " (Matthew 25:34–36). The righteous will question when they ever saw Him in any of these conditions and ministered to Him. He will reply, " 'Truly I say to you, to the extent that you did it to one of these brothers of Mine, even the least of them, you did it to Me' " (Matthew 25:40).

I have one brother, and by definition we are brothers because we share the same parents. Who are Christ's brothers? They are the ones who are sons of the same Father. Jesus is the Son of God, and when we become part of Him, His designation as the Son of God also becomes our designation. If both we and Jesus are sons of the Father, then by definition this makes us brothers with Jesus. These are the "brothers" to whom Jesus referred when He said, " ' "To the extent that you did it to one of these brothers of Mine, even the least of them, you did it to Me." ' " Jesus considers acts done to any of His brothers as done to Him. No matter how weak or insignificant a person may seem to be, if that person has the Spirit of Christ dwelling in his heart, then he is part of Christ. Whatever befalls that person also befalls Christ. If that person is mistreated, Christ is mistreated. If someone does a kind deed to that person, the kind deed was, of a truth, done to Christ.

When we treat these brothers of Christ kindly, we are treating Christ kindly. On the flip side, Jesus will reject those who neglected to care for Him, saying, " ' "Truly I say to you, to the extent that you did not do it to one of the least of these, you did not do it to Me" ' " (Matthew 25:45). Therefore, the way we mistreat those who have Christ's Spirit dwelling within them is the way that we mistreat Christ Himself.

You may remember that young Saul had received authority from the Jewish leaders in Jerusalem to go and persecute the Christians in Damascus. While he was on the way, a great light shone about him, and he fell to the ground. When he heard a voice speaking to him, did the voice say, "Saul, Saul, why are you persecuting My church?" No, the voice said, " 'Saul, Saul, why are you persecuting Me?' " (Acts 9:4). Saul then replied, " 'Who are You, Lord?' " The voice responded, " 'I am Jesus whom you are persecuting' " (verse 5).

Jesus considered Saul's persecution of His people as being done to Him. Jesus once said, "Whoever receives one child like this in My name receives Me" (Mark 9:37a). As we have studied, Jesus is one with the Father. Therefore He goes on to say, " 'And whoever receives Me does not receive Me, but Him who sent Me' " (37b). How we treat fellow believers, then, is truly important.

The school I attended when I was in sixth grade had a large asphalt parking lot behind it that was used for overflow parking during big events. When it was empty, our class would use it sometimes during recess. One particular day we were playing kickball on the parking lot. I was in the outfield, and somebody kicked the ball in my direction. As I was backing up to catch the ball, somehow I tangled my ungainly feet beneath me, and when I reached out to catch myself, the impact sent a searing pain up my arm. Recess for me was over. When the teacher saw me leaping around in pain in the outfield, she decided recess was over not only for me but for everybody.

We filed back into the classroom, and the teacher called my mother, who soon arrived and took me to the hospital. The clinicians did an X-ray of my arm, and, sure enough, it was broken. They put a splint on it, gave me some pain medication, and then, a few days later, they put a hard cast on it. These medical professionals were not just treating my arm. They were treating me, for my arm is part of me. In the same way, when Christ makes us part of His body, whatever happens to us happens to Him. If people care for members of His body, they are caring for Him.

The Second Greatest Commandment Is Like the First

With respect to fellow believers, in a special sense it can be said that the second greatest commandment is like the first. When someone loves a follower of Christ, that person is showing love to Christ.

You may remember the story of the man who came to Jesus to test Him, saying, " 'Teacher, which is the great commandment in the Law?' " (Matthew 22:36).

Jesus replied, " 'You shall love the Lord your God with all your heart, and with all your soul, and with all your mind' " (verse 37). Then Jesus volunteered some additional information: " 'The second is like it. You shall love your neighbor as yourself' " (verse 39). When we love members of Christ's body, we are fulfilling not only the second greatest commandment but also the greatest commandment, which says, "Love the Lord your God with all of your heart, soul, mind, and strength."

John emphasized the point when he wrote, "Whoever believes that Jesus is the Christ is born of God, and whoever loves the Father loves the child born of Him" (1 John 5:1). Whoever counts Jesus to be worth obeying and passionately presses on to know and do His will—that person is born of God. They also love those who accept Jesus as the ruler of their lives. If they internalize Jesus' words, then they have God's Spirit dwelling within them. Therefore, to not love them would be to not love God in the form of the Holy Spirit.

Jesus said, " 'Where two or three have gathered together in My name, I am there in their midst' " (Matthew 18:20). When we are one with Him, Christ is there in the person of the other ones present. If you have the Spirit of Christ dwelling within you, then when I gather with you, I am meeting with Christ, because He is dwelling in your heart. Based on these clues, we can see that the way we treat other believers is the way we treat Christ.

We become members of Christ, and Christ is the head of the body. We should treat one another as members of His body, but He is the authority over us all. Never should we give worship to one another or receive it from others.

A Hindu friend once said to me, "In our culture we greet one another with a bow. The custom originated because people were bowing to the god inside the other person." Even in the Christian Church, some have been swept directly into that error. And even if they do not go that far, many bow to religious leaders, whether pope, priest, or pastor. Christ only is our head. All of us are fellow members of His body, and we should relate to one another as equals. Jesus instructed,

"Do not be called Rabbi; for One is your Teacher, and you are all brothers. Do not call anyone on earth your father; for One is your Father, He who is in heaven. Do not be called leaders; for One is your Leader, that is, Christ" (Matthew 23:8–10).

Never in matters of conscience should we yield our decisions to someone else, and never should we stand as an intermediary between any other person and God. A direct link must exist between the head and each member of His body. That said, this truth does not negate the reality that Christ considers things done to His followers as done to Himself. Therefore we should act accordingly.

What About Brothers Who Do Not Act Christ-like?

It is important to realize that the way we treat fellow believers is the way that we treat Christ even when they are not acting Christ-like. Jesus took upon Himself our infirmities. He made us members of Himself while we were still filled with sinful propensities. He is working to purify us, but He is not done yet. It is possible that someone can be fully committed to knowing and doing God's will but still be ignorant of some of His teachings. Furthermore, although we desire to fully conform to God's will, we are all still liable to err and make mistakes along the way. Christ does not cast us off every time we fail; rather He installed a safety net to catch us, restore us, and help us get up and press on again to His high calling.

Sanctification is a life-long process. Hebrews 12:14 says, "Pursue peace with all men, and the sanctification without which no one will see the Lord." If sanctification must be pursued, then it does not happen in a moment. Therefore, if somebody is acting un-Christ-like to us, that does not mean they have ceased being part of Christ's body. Christ took our infirmities upon Himself, and our sin was laid upon Him.

Christ and our sin mix for a little while until He has had time to cleanse the temple of His body from all sin. Therefore the way we treat a fellow believer is the way we treat Christ, however poorly that person may be acting.

I have been in a few church meetings that have turned openly hostile. If you attend a church board meeting and it gets a little hot, remember that those who oppose you are still members of Christ, and even though they may not be acting Christ-like at the moment, the way you treat them is the way you treat Christ. If your husband or wife says something with a bite, be ever so careful how you respond. If your child loses his temper, know that if he has expressed a commitment to Christ, then the way you treat Him is the way you treat Christ.

Members of One Another

When Jesus' Spirit is living within you and He is living within me, the Bible says this makes us members of one another. Paul wrote, "For just as we have many members in one body and all the members do not have the same function, so we, who are many, are one body in Christ, and individually members one of another" (Romans 12:4, 5). And John the apostle wrote, "What we have seen and heard we proclaim to you also, so that you too may have fellowship with us; and indeed our fellowship is with the Father, and with His son Jesus Christ" (1 John 1:3). We have studied the amazing fellowship we can have with God—how we can be one with Jesus and one with the Father. But these texts indicate that it is not just unity with the Father and with Jesus that we can have, but also unity with one another. The same level of unity that we can have with the Father and the Son is the level of unity He wants to see between fellow believers. Our fellowship is with anyone who has the Holy Spirit—the Father, the Son, and fellow followers of Christ.

A few years ago, my wife and I were driving to a family

reunion near the Great Smoky Mountains National Park. We were traveling along country roads when suddenly the car started to sputter and stumble and misfire. I thought to myself, *Oh no, here we are, many miles from the nearest civilization. Now what are going to do?* We limped along as best as we could and finally came into a town. The car stalled at one point, and we had to get it jump-started to get it going again. At last, an auto parts store appeared on the left-hand side of the road. The car almost stalled out again in the turning lane, but with some careful nursing we made it into the store parking lot. One of the store employees helped me read the engine codes, and he said, "You have a coolant temperature sensor that has gone bad." The new sensor cost about $20, and the old sensor was located right at the top of the engine. It only took a couple of minutes to replace, and then the car worked wonderfully.

The components of an engine make up a full system. It could be said that they are members of one another because they are part of the system. The crankshaft cannot work properly if the coolant temperature sensor malfunctions. The same is true of the pistons, transmission, and wheels. All these components are needed in order to make a complete system. They are members of one another. In like manner, those who are members of Christ's body are members of one another. Each of us needs every other member.

Loving the Non-Christian

In this chapter we are emphasizing the special care that we should have for members of Christ's body. But it should be noted that the kindness we show should not be limited to those who are members of Christ's body. We should be kind and loving to all people, even to those who are our enemies, whether they are part of the body of Christ or not. While we were still sinners, enemies of Christ, He died for us. He is our example. I like the way Paul summed it up in Galatians 6:10: "While we have an opportunity let us do good to all people, and especially to those who are of the household of faith." Just as our heavenly Father sends the sun and the rain on the good and the bad, we also should be kind to anybody with whom we come in contact.

The Source of Unity Among Believers

Unity among believers is critically important. That unity comes from putting aside our differences. Stay with me here. It does not come by putting aside our doctrinal differences but by putting aside our differences with God. It comes by becoming one with God. Those who share His Spirit will naturally be united with one another. We should exercise Christian courtesy and give preference to one another in non-doctrinal matters. The color of the church carpet is not worth becoming divided over. But when it comes to doctrine, the way to have unity is not by focusing on the unity itself but by coming close to Christ. Becoming united with Christ draws us to one another.

Paul gave some solid counsel to the Ephesians when he wrote,

[God] gave some as apostles, and some as prophets, and some as evangelists, and some as pastors and teachers, for the equipping of the saints for the work of service, to the building up of the body of Christ; until we all attain to the unity of the faith, and of the knowledge of the Son of God, to a mature man, to the measure of the stature which belongs to the fullness of Christ (4:11–13).

Note that unity comes from building up the body of Christ by equipping them with knowledge of the Son of God. In other words, unity comes from knowing and living out the truth.

Paul goes on, describing the source of this unity.

As a result, we are no longer to be children, tossed here and there by waves and carried about by every wind of doctrine, by the trickery of men, by craftiness in deceitful scheming; but speaking the truth in love, we are to grow up in all aspects into Him who is the head, even Christ (4:14, 15).

Unity comes from speaking the truth in love; it comes by observing sound doctrine; it comes from finding and applying the truth in our lives.

Northeast of San Francisco is the Shiloh Wind Farm, with almost three hundred wind turbines. One time Amy and I drove through the middle of it, and it was like driving through a forest of giant pinwheels. The structures are huge, some with a hub height of more than 260 feet and a rotor diameter of more than three hundred feet, making the total height more than four hundred feet. The rotors protrude expansively from the hub, yet as you get closer to the hub, those rotors get closer together. That is the way it is with Christ. He is like that hub, and we are like the rotors. As we come closer to Him, we come closer to one another.

In the back part of Joshua Tree National Park are some abandoned gold mines. When the mines were in operation, the miners knew that if they wanted to get the gold out of the rock, they could not pick at the rock with hand tools. If they did so, they would go bankrupt in the process. It was not cost-effective to gather the gold flecks and nuggets directly out of the veins of quartz and other rock. Therefore the gold miners dragged massive pieces of equipment out into the desert. You can still see some of them out there today. They took the gold ore and crushed it into fine powder, ran it through additional processes using mercury, of all things, and at the end they collected the pure gold. They focused on the process, and, at the end, out came the gold. In like manner, if we want unity among the people of God, we need to focus on having unity with Christ. If we focus on that process, then the unity among fellow believers will be the outflow from it.

Costly Love

This love that Christ desires us to exhibit to one another will cost us something. In 1 John 3:16, the apostle beloved of Jesus wrote, "We know love by this, that He laid down His life for us; and we ought to lay down our lives for the brethren." What does it mean to lay down our lives for our brothers? It means that we give up our lives for those who believe in Jesus. It tangibly costs us something to love others—it decreases our life. Love is expressed in action. Just a simple affectionate feeling toward someone is not worth much, but actions done for the sake of benefitting the other person are what really count.

Good works usually require some sort of sacrifice—exertion, sweat, difficulty, pain, resources, or time. When we are finished, we may be tired, poor, and dirty. We may have lost out on other things we enjoy doing. We may feel spent emotionally and spiritually. Our efforts may even go unrecognized. But in the end, this giving of ourselves is what it means to lay down our lives for the brothers of Christ.

One time I shared some of these thoughts in a church near my home. One of the members came up to me afterward. He knew that we had recently moved to the area, and I was still trying to find a good used riding mower to care for our yard. In the meantime our grass had gotten out of hand. The man said, "I would like to come help you mow your yard tomorrow."

I thought to myself, *Oh no, I did not mean to sound like I was manipulating people to serve me.* He was very genuine, though, and I finally decided the very best thing I could do was to let him lavish love on us. He came about 10:00 A.M. the next day, and we worked on that yard together. He finally left at about 6:00 P.M. He sacrificed almost his whole day for me.

He was sweaty and dusty and tired, he had used his gas, and he had put wear and tear on his machines. In the process, he preached my sermon over again more eloquently than I could ever have put it, because he demonstrated it with his actions.

Fervent Love

We should not just love our brothers, we should love them fervently. Peter counseled, "Since you have in obedience to the truth purified your souls for a sincere love of the brethren, fervently love one another from the heart" (1 Peter 1:22). The level of love that Peter refers to here is not just an occasional sacrifice but an ongoing sacrifice, where we sustain very real losses multiple times a day. This level of sacrifice is seen when a mother nurses her baby every three hours through the night, washes his laundry, bathes him, changes his diapers, and endures being spit up on. She does all of this at immense expense to her own time, fun, and money, and the baby cannot even express gratitude. However, she loves her baby. She may bend over the crib and whisper, "I love you," but her love goes far beyond mere words. Her love is an example of the type of love John referred to when he wrote, "Let us not love with word or with tongue, but in deed and truth" (1 John 3:18).

This type of service is the true measure of greatness. Jesus declared, " 'The greatest among you shall be your servant' " (Matthew 23:11). We serve others every time we give of our lives for them—every time we sacrifice things that are meaningful to us in order to benefit them.

A Great Gift

One of the greatest ways we can serve is by helping one another overcome sin. The night before Jesus was crucified, He took off His outer garment, dressed Himself as a servant, and poured water in a basin. Then He knelt down in front of the travel-weary disciples and began to wash their feet. Peter, however, did not like the idea of Jesus being the servant, and he said, " 'Lord, do You wash my feet?' " (John 13:6). He called Him "Lord." He did not want Jesus to be the servant. He emphatically declared, " 'Never shall You wash my feet!' " (verse 8a).

Jesus replied, " 'If I do not wash you, you have no part with Me' " (verse 8b). This act included more than Jesus washing the feet of the disciples. He was trying to teach a deeper lesson. Of course, Peter quickly backtracked on his statement and allowed Jesus to wash his feet. Jesus washed the rest of the disciples' feet, and then he sat down and asked something very interesting: " 'Do you know what I have done to you?' " (verse 12). Jesus was here indicating that what He had done was not as obvious as washing their feet. He said, " 'If I then, the Lord and the Teacher, washed your feet, you also ought to wash one another's feet' " (verse 14).

He was trying to show how He washes His disciples with the Word. The physical ceremony of baptism is a symbol of how we die to our old way of life and how we are raised to a new way of life. In other words, we no longer respond to our old evil habits, but we do respond to the Spirit's desires. When we embrace this change in attitude, Christ forgives us from all our past sins. After this initial cleansing, He continues to work with us, helping us to overcome whatever sinful tendencies might remain in our hearts. He washes us on an ongoing basis. He washes us with the Word. In like manner, we too are to wash one another's feet.

Jesus did not just point at the disciples' feet and say, "Your feet are dirty." He washed the disciples' feet, and that is what we should do as well. We are to embrace the inconvenience, the difficulty, and the burden of helping others overcome sin.

A mother was physically and verbally abusive to her daughter. Her fellow church members saw what was happening. One of the women eventually confronted her about it. She suggested to the angry mother that she send the rebellious girl to a reform school. The child would have help dealing with her rebellion, and the mother would have a more favorable situation in which to work on her anger problems. The mother found the option attractive, but she could not afford the full tuition. The woman who had done the confronting went home and discussed the options with her husband. They sold a piece of property they owned, and they used the money to pay the tuition difference for the girl to attend the school. Such is what it means to wash one another's feet. You and I should wash one another's feet just as Jesus washes our feet.

If a fellow Christian falls into an obvious sin, we should gently restore that person. Paul wrote,

> Brethren, even if anyone is caught in any trespass, you who are spiritual, restore such a one in a spirit of gentleness; each one looking to yourself, so that you too will not be tempted. Bear one another's burdens, and thereby fulfill the law of Christ (Galatians 6:1, 2).

What does it mean to bear one another's burdens? As the text says, it means to gently restore another when they are caught in a sin; this is what it means to wash one another's feet.

We in our churches tend to shoot our wounded. In war it does not happen that way. Early in World War II, the Japanese invaded the Philippines. They overwhelmed the American forces and took tens of thousands of them as prisoners. In 1944 General MacArthur set about to recapture those islands. One of the Japanese prison camps was at a place called Cabanatuan. At the peak of the war it housed several thousand POWs. As the American forces advanced, the Japanese transferred all the healthy prisoners back to Japan to work in forced labor camps there. They left all the sickly, dying, weak ones at the camp in Cabanatuan. The Americans were very concerned about those remaining prisoners because as American forces advanced on other prison camps, the Japanese had been known to kill the prisoners rather than risk having the Americans recover them, rehabilitate them, and send them back to fight.

The Americans approached to within thirty miles of the camp, and they decided that the need to help the POWs was critical. A group of 120 Army Rangers along with eighty Filipino guerillas headed off, hiking through the back country to attempt a rescue. There were two hundred guards in the Japanese camp and another thousand or so Japanese soldiers across a nearby river. It was two hundred against twelve hundred. As the allied force approached the camp's outskirts, they surveyed the situation and carefully planned how they would take on that number of enemy soldiers. They set up a road block across the river, and then the Rangers approached the camp. They started the attack in the evening after sundown, so that the guards would not see them creeping across the grassy area that surrounded the camp. Within the first fifteen seconds of combat, they had destroyed all the guard shacks and the pillbox bunkers that guarded the camp. Within thirty-five minutes, every single prisoner was free. Then they turned right around, because they were still on enemy territory, and started back those thirty miles.[6]

Those soldiers who carried out the rescue had only slept five or six hours in three days; they walked sixty miles and risked their lives—all for men who were weak, sickly, and who did not recognize them due to the new uniforms the Army had issued during the three years since they had been taken captive. The prisoners had hidden in the bunkhouses and in the latrines and in the ditches, terrified of those who

---

6. Adapted from the story told in William E. Breuer, *The Great Raid on Cabanatuan: Rescuing the Doomed Ghosts of Bataan and Corregidor* (New York: Wiley, 1994).

had invaded the camp. All of these sacrifices and all of this work were expended to rescue diseased, weak, starving POWs who would cost money and resources to rehabilitate.

If these soldiers endured that kind of hardship to rescue POWs, how much more should our churches seek to rescue those who have fallen under Satan's temptations! Let's not write people off just because they are struggling. Let's call in the helicopters. Let's call in the reinforcements. We should stop at nothing to restore and build up a fallen fellow Christian.

True, there are times that those who need help refuse it. Only after we have entreated that person privately, then with one or two others, then with the whole church, and they still do not listen, should they be separated from the church. Even at that point, the separation should come for the sake of rousing the person to a sense of their need. This world is very dangerous to our spiritual interests, and we need to watch one another's back in case any of us are trapped by sin's deceitfulness.

Paul wrote of a man in the Corinthian Church: "There is immorality among you, and immorality of such a kind as does not exist even among the Gentiles." This man was having an affair with his father's wife, probably a stepmother. Paul told them,

> In the name of our Lord Jesus, when you are assembled, and I with you in spirit, with the power of our Lord Jesus, I have decided to deliver such a one to Satan for the destruction of his flesh, so that his spirit may be saved in the day of the Lord Jesus (1 Corinthians 5:1, 4, 5).

Notice carefully that the discipline was for the sake of the erring one to be saved. And it worked, because in the next letter we read how Paul was encouraging them to restore this man so that he would not be overwhelmed with too much sorrow (2 Corinthians 2:7). That should be our attitude. Let's restore people and build them up.

The Definitive Proof of a Christian

In our Christian experience, self-sacrificial love for other people is where the rubber meets the road. If we set our hearts to know and do God's will, love is where it shows up in actual practice. As we touched on in chapter 3, love is the definitive proof that God's Word is working in our hearts. John the apostle wrote, "We know that we have passed out of death into life, because we love the brethren" (1 John 3:14). The brethren are the brothers of Christ, those who are sons of the Father, and love for these brothers of Christ is the proof that we have passed out of death into life. John continued, "If we love one another God abides in us, and His love is perfected in us" (verse 12).

Paul corrected the believers in Corinth because they lacked this love for one another. When they gathered to celebrate the Lord's Supper, some were indulging themselves while others who had nothing went without. Each person was looking out for his own needs and not the needs of others. Paul wrote,

> What shall I say to you? Shall I praise you? In this I will not praise you. For I received from the Lord that which I also delivered to you, that the Lord Jesus in the night in which He was betrayed took bread; and when He had given thanks, He broke it and said, "This is My body, which is for you; do this in remembrance of Me." In the same way He took the cup also after supper, saying, "This cup is the new covenant in My blood; do this, as often as you drink it, in remembrance of Me" (1 Corinthians 11:22–25).

The bread and blood of the grape were ways to remember Jesus; they were symbols of His teaching. They were also symbols of His Spirit. When a person takes in the symbols of Jesus' body and blood, he is saying, in essence, that he is part of Christ; he claims that he is a person who internalizes Jesus' words and Spirit. Paul was concerned because those who claimed to internalize Jesus' words and Spirit were not acting according to their profession. He warned, "Therefore whoever eats the bread or drinks the cup of the Lord in an unworthy manner, shall be guilty of the body and the blood of the Lord" (verse 27).

A bulimic person takes in food but then purges it before it can be digested. That food is wasted. In the same way, if someone claims to take in the teaching and Spirit of Jesus but then does not act accordingly, he in effect vomits the teaching out. That teaching is wasted upon him, and consequently he is guilty of doing violence to Jesus. Before partaking of the symbols of Jesus' body and blood, before making a claim that we are a person who internalizes His teaching and Spirit, we should each examine ourselves to make sure that we have aligned ourselves to everything we know is His will.

We should take pains to be considerate of fellow believers, watching out for and meeting their needs. Paul wrote about those who partake of the symbol of Christ's body and blood, saying,

> Is not the cup of blessing which we bless a sharing in the blood of Christ? Is not the bread which we break a sharing in the body of Christ? Since there is one bread, we who are many are one body; for we all partake of the one bread (1 Corinthians 10:16, 17).

Paul here emphasized the point that those who internalize Jesus' teaching are Christ's body. If someone acts thoughtlessly toward their fellow believers, in so doing they fail to discern Christ's body. Someone who partakes of the symbols of Christ's body and yet treats his actual body with contempt shows that Christ's teaching, which he claims to have internalized, has not yet sunk deep enough in his heart.

Similarly, Paul wrote about the Lord's Supper: "He who eats and drinks, eats and drinks judgment to himself if he does not judge the body rightly" (1 Corinthians 11:29). Then he concluded, "So then, My brethren, when you come together to eat, wait for one another. If anyone is hungry, let him eat at home, so that you will not come together for judgment" (verses 33, 34). Here is where the rubber meets the road. Love for Christ's brethren is where keeping Jesus' words shows up in practical life. "If we love one another, God abides in us, and His love is perfected in us" (1 John 4:12).

We show love to God by showing love to those who are members of His body. So remember, when the Holy Spirit is within you, the way I treat you is the way Christ considers that I treated him; and when the Holy Spirit is within you and the Holy Spirit is also within me, then the way I treat you is the way I treat myself. I would like to challenge each of us to come up with ways that we can lay down our lives for one another. How can we benefit another follower of Christ, even if it tangibly decreases our life?

Loving Christ

We would all do well to prayerfully consider the passage in 1 Corinthians 13 about love and identify at least one thing from this passage that we can use to benefit someone else, even at the expense of decreasing our own lives. There Paul wrote, "Love is patient, love is kind and is not jealous; love does not brag and is not arrogant, does not act unbecomingly; it does not seek its own, is not provoked" (verses 4, 5). I could apply that in my own life, practicing patience with my kids. I am not there yet, but by God's grace I am pressing forward. "[Love] does not take into account a wrong suffered, does not rejoice in unrighteousness, but rejoices with the truth; bears all things, believes all things, hopes all things, endures all things. Love never fails" (verses 5–8). This call is that we lay down our lives for the benefit of Christ's body. Let's whole-heartedly embrace the sacrifice.

Discussion Questions:

1. What is the source of unity among believers?

2. What is the definitive proof of a person being a Christian?

3. Explain what it means for a person to be a brother of Christ. How does one become a brother of Christ?

4. Explain in your own words the significant lesson Jesus tried to convey when He washed the disciples' feet.

5. Sketch a verbal picture of what it means to lay down one's life for the brethren.

6. Share an example of bearing one another's burdens. The example could be from your own life or from the life of a friend.

7. This chapter focused on the importance of loving the brothers of Christ with a special love. Identify at least three additional reasons it is important to love all people, including our enemies.

8. Think of a time when you have been hurt by someone who professed to be a member of Christ's body but acted contrary to that profession. How did you handle the situation? Recognizing that Christ views that individual as part of Himself, even though faulty, would you do anything differently if you were able to go back in time and handle the situation over again? If so, what would you change?

9. How does one love from the heart and also set appropriate boundaries when it comes to deeply damaging actions such as child sexual abuse, physical abuse, or substance abuse? How are love and boundaries interconnected?

10. Think of a fellow believer's situation that you would rather ignore. Remember that the way we treat a fellow believer is the way we treat ourselves because we are members of one another. Develop a plan for serving "yourself" in the person of the one who needs help.

11. Compare and contrast the unity we can have with God, and the unity we can have with fellow believers. How are they similar? How are they different?

12. Just because someone becomes part of Christ does not mean they become the head of the body. How is the way we interact with fellow believers similar to how we interact with Christ as the head, and how is it different?

Part 2

The Message of the Kingdom

CHAPTER SIX

The Message of the Kingdom

The 121-year-old San José copper and gold mine is located in the Atacama Desert in Chile. On August 5, 2010, a block of rock twice as big as the Empire State Building broke free and collapsed the main tunnel, sealing it off three miles from the mine entrance. Authorities on the surface believed that men deep in the mine might have survived the cave-in. The mine owners began drilling eight exploratory boreholes into different regions of the mine to see if there were any signs of life.

One of those boreholes was aimed at a section of the mine with an emergency station that miners called the Refuge, with the hope that the trapped men might have congregated there. Seventeen days after the cave-in, the drill bit broke through into that chamber. When the rescue workers at the surface withdrew the bit, taped to the end of it was a note in bold red letters that said, "We are well, the 33 of us."

That exploratory borehole was just a few inches in diameter, and the chamber was 2,300 feet below the surface. Food and medicine could be passed down the hole, but no person could fit through it. A larger tunnel had to be dug in order to rescue the men. Eventually the government took over the rescue operation, bringing in big machines capable of drilling holes wide enough to get the men out.

Sixty-nine days after the men were first trapped, one of those large drilling rigs broke through into the chamber where they were waiting. The rescue began, bringing the men up in a capsule just big enough for one person to squeeze into. Probably most who read this chapter remember those iconic images and videos as, one by one, the men were brought to the surface—the emotional reunions with family members, the elation of being free from their underground prison, and the heartfelt thanks they expressed to the rescuers.[7]

Media sources estimated that more than a billion people watched live as those men were rescued. One-seventh of the world's population watched over a period of about twenty-four hours.[8] The technology we have to communicate is unparalleled in the history of this world, making it possible that in one day, this message could go to a billion people.

Jesus spoke about a message that would go to the whole world as a witness and then the end would come. The disciples came to Jesus and asked Him about the signs of His coming, of the end of the age and the destruction of Jerusalem. He began to tell some of the things that they should watch out for. He said, " 'Many will come in My name, saying, "I am the Christ," and will mislead many' " (Matthew 24:5). Jesus prophesied that many would claim to come in His name, to be one with Him, when in truth they are not

7. Bob Simons, "Chilean Miners Rescued, But Were They Saved?" *CBS News*, Feb. 10, 2011, http://www.cbsnews.com/news/chilean-miners-rescued-but-were-they-saved-10-02-2011/.

8. Rosa Flores and Michelle Rozsa, "What You Might Not Know About the Chilean Mine Rescue," *CNN*, Aug. 4, 2015, http://www.cnn.com/2015/08/03/world/chilean-miners-surprising-facts/.

part of Him. These are the ones who make a profession of Christ but do not submit their lives to Him. They draw near to Him with their lips, but their hearts are far from Him.

Jesus continued,

"You will be hearing of wars and rumors of wars. See that you are not frightened, for these things must take place, but that is not yet the end. For nation will rise against nation, and kingdom against kingdom, and in various places there will be famines and earthquakes. But all of these things are merely the beginning of birth pangs" (verses 6–8).

These signs, though, are not the end. Yes, they are signs, but "that is not yet the end." A few verses later Jesus shared the one sign that, when it happens, will signify that the end actually is upon us. He said, "This gospel of the kingdom shall be preached in the whole world as a testimony to them and then the end will come" (verse 14).

If you ask people to define the kingdom of God, you will get a wide variety of answers. Some say it is the church. Others say it is heaven. Still others say it is a method of world evangelism. This confusion raises a haunting question. How can we preach the gospel of the kingdom if we have trouble defining the kingdom?

Jesus' prophecy about the gospel of the kingdom going to the whole world is unfulfilled, I believe, not so much because we lack the ability to communicate with the whole world—remember, a billion people were reached in one day with the message of the Chilean mine rescue—but because most Christians are sharing an incomplete message. We must share the gospel again with every nation, tribe, language, and people, this time declaring the truth of unity with Christ through internalizing His teachings.

The Eternal Gospel

Since it is so important to share this gospel of the kingdom, what are the essential elements that must be shared? The first angel's message in Revelation 14:6 contains an embedded summary of the eternal gospel. John records, "I saw another angel flying in midheaven, having an eternal gospel to preach to those who live on the earth." Are you ready to hear the eternal gospel that this angel bears? " 'Fear God, and give glory to Him . . . [and] worship Him' " (verse 7). This message is the eternal gospel stripped down to the essential element that we must act on. It is a message about an attitude of obedience. Wherever this message has been preached, the gospel of the kingdom has been shared.

Two Dangerous Pitfalls

Recently I was talking with some people at a study group, and the subject of obedience to God came up. Interestingly the group was polarized. Some said, "God's grace covers all your sins, so you need not be overly concerned about obedience." Then others said, "No, obedience is crucial." One of the men, previously a minister, lamented the fact that in many popular churches if you mention the word *obedience* you are liable to be escorted out as a legalist. As we have studied, our part in the plan of salvation is to have an attitude of obedience, depending on Christ for strength. Therefore the tendency to equate an attitude of obedience with legalism eclipses our part in the plan of salvation, making it far more difficult to find the narrow gate and straight way that leads to eternal life.

Another equally dangerous pitfall exists of which we must be wary: some think they must get their lives right before they come to Jesus. They set about to clean up this or that area of their lives, and sometimes they may even have some outward success. They think that by piling up a certain number of good works that outweigh their bad works they will somehow earn the right to enter heaven. However, only God can change the heart. We must never forget that the gospel of the kingdom is a message about unity with Christ. This message is not about separation from Christ while we feebly attempt to do the impossible task of purifying our own hearts. Jesus cleansed the temple of old, and it is still Jesus who cleanses the temple of the heart today. We must come to Christ just as we are, loaded down with sins and faults, but with a decision to obey, depending on Him for strength. He will then work in us to enable us to do what is right.

Most of Christianity has fallen into one or the other of these two errors. Many speak of the eternal life Jesus offers, but they remove the very core of our part in the plan of salvation—an attitude of obedience. Many others speak of the necessity of obedience, but they remove the very core of God's part in the plan of salvation—the Holy Spirit dwelling within a person, giving the desire and ability to do what is right. The prevalence of these two errors is the major reason the kingdom of God, I believe, has not been fully preached.

When we make the connection that the kingdom of God is another way of describing unity with Christ, then we can apply the ideas we have learned about unity with Christ to our understanding of the kingdom of God. We have already studied in previous chapters the all-important attitude required to enter into unity with Christ, an attitude of wholeheartedly seeking to know and do God's will, depending on Him for strength. We have also studied the resulting unity with God that flows from that attitude, where God causes His Holy Spirit to dwell within us, giving us the desire and ability to do what is right. These same principles apply to the kingdom of God. Such an understanding dispels both the error that we can obtain salvation without a headlong pursuit of God's will, and the error that we can obtain salvation by our own efforts. It also brings into sharp focus the elements required to enter the kingdom of God. Thus it prepares us to truly share the gospel of the kingdom. Therefore, let's look at some of the clues that the gospel of the kingdom and the message of unity with Christ are one and the same.

Clue 1: The Entrance Requirement

The first clue is the entrance requirement to the kingdom and to the body. Jesus declared,

> "Not everyone who says to Me, 'Lord, Lord,' will enter the kingdom of heaven, but He who does the will of My Father who is in heaven will enter. Many will say to Me on that day, 'Lord, Lord, did we not prophesy in Your name, and in Your name cast out demons, and in Your name perform many miracles?' And then I will declare to them, 'I never knew you; depart from Me, you who practice lawlessness' " (Matthew 7:21–23).

According to this text, the entrance requirement into the kingdom is that we do the will of the Father. The requirement is the same for entrance into Jesus' body. Jesus compared it to a vine and its branches, saying,

> "Abide in Me, and I in you. As the branch cannot bear fruit unless it abides in the vine, so neither can you, unless you abide in Me. . . . If you keep My commandments, you will abide in My love even as I have kept My Father's commandments and abide in His love" (John 15:4, 10).

This declaration tells us that the entrance requirement into unity with Christ is that we keep His commandments. Jesus came to do the Father's will, and therefore His commands are an expression of the Father's will. So the entrance requirement into the body is the same as the entrance requirement into the kingdom—to do the Father's will. The type of submission He requires is not just a mere compliance with God's commands, but it is the wholehearted attitude of obedience we have already discussed.

Some years ago I was searching for a new job, and I wanted to get into full-time work designing medical devices. In the search I became familiar with the major medical device companies across the United States. One day an independent recruiter e-mailed me and shared the requirements for a job opportunity without disclosing the company name. He explained that it was for a major medical device manufacturer in the Intermountain Region,[9] and the responsibilities were in catheter design. After reading the description, I thought to myself, *I believe I know which company that is.* When I checked the company's website, the same job description was posted there. Now, the recruiter did not want me to know the name of the company because sometimes candidates will go around the recruiter and apply directly to the company, and then the recruiter may not get paid. But I wanted to know who I might be applying to before spending lots of time pursuing an opportunity. The requirements listed for that job on the website were the same as the requirements the recruiter had sent me; therefore, I knew that both described the same position.

The same idea applies when it comes to the entrance requirements to the kingdom versus the entrance requirements to the body of Christ. The requirements are one and the same. It is a clue that the kingdom of God is the body of Christ.

Clue 2: The Location

The second clue is the location. Jesus said, " 'The kingdom of God does not come with observation; nor will they say, "See here!" or "See there!" For indeed, the kingdom of God is within you' " (Luke 17:20, 21, NKJV). The location of the kingdom of God is within you. The same idea defines the body of Christ. Paul described the body when he wrote, "We are the temple of the living God; just as God said, 'I will dwell in them

---

9. The western United States region between the Rocky Mountains and the Sierra Nevada.

and walk among them; and I will be their God, and they shall be My people' " (2 Corinthians 6:16).

We have studied how Jesus is the temple for His Father. He said, " 'Destroy this temple, and in three days I will raise it up' " (John 2:19). And as John pointed out, "He was speaking of the temple of His body" (verse 21). He was the temple for His Father. When we are joined to Christ in Spirit, then we become part of the temple for the Father—the temple for the Holy Spirit dwelling in our hearts. Therefore the location of the kingdom is within us; likewise the location of this experience of oneness with God is within us.

When I transferred from a job in California to one in Memphis, Tennessee, my employer helped us move. The company paid to ship our belongings, including our cars, and we flew to the new location. When the freight company was trying to figure out a place to drop the vehicles for us in Memphis, I gave them my new work address. They looked it up on their map and said, "Oh, we do not have that address. Our system shows a different address for the place where you work." As it turned out, the street name had been changed. Both addresses referred to the very same location. With the kingdom of God and the body of Christ it is the same. The terms used to describe them are different, but the location is the same.

Clue 3: The Authority Structure

The third clue is the authority structure laid out in these two messages. God gave Daniel a vision regarding the kingdom. He described a splendid judgment scene where the Ancient of Days was presiding. Then he said,

"I kept looking in the night visions, and behold, with the clouds of heaven one like a Son of Man was coming, and He came up to the Ancient of Days and was presented before Him. And to Him was given dominion, glory and a kingdom, that all the peoples, nations and men of every language might serve Him. His dominion is an everlasting dominion which will not pass away; and His kingdom is one which will not be destroyed. . . . Then the sovereignty, the dominion and the greatness of all the kingdoms under the whole heaven will be given to the people of the saints of the Highest One; His kingdom will be an everlasting kingdom, and all the dominions will serve and obey Him" (Daniel 7:13, 14, 27).

The Father is described here with several names. He is "The Ancient of Days," "The Most High," and "The Highest One." He gave a kingdom to Jesus, who is one "like a Son of Man." In turn Jesus eventually gave that kingdom to those who follow God. Notice the authority structure established here. The Father delegated authority to Jesus, and Jesus delegated authority to believers. The one who delegates authority is ruler over the one to whom He delegates. While verse 14 says the kingdom was given to Jesus, verse 27 describes that same kingdom as being of "The Highest One," which is the Father.

Paul described that authority structure in the kingdom this way:

Then comes the end, when He hands over the kingdom to the God and Father, when He has abolished all rule and all authority and power. For He must reign until He has put all His enemies under His feet. The last enemy that will be abolished is death. For He has put all things in subjection under His feet. But when He says, "All things are put in subjection," it is evident that He is excepted who put all things in subjection to Him. When all things are subjected to Him, then the Son Himself also will be subjected to the One who subjected all things to Him, so that God may be all in all (1 Corinthians 15:24–28).

Paul described the same authority structure in the body of Christ. Speaking of Christ he wrote,

He [the Father] raised Him from the dead and seated Him at His right hand in the heavenly places, far above all rule and authority and power and dominion, and every name that is named, not only in this age but also in the one to come. And He put all things in subjection under His feet, and gave Him as head over all things to the church, which is His body, the fullness of Him who fills all in all (Ephesians 1:20–23).

The dominion given to Christ was the role of being the head of the body. Paul succinctly summed it up, writing, "I want you to understand that Christ is the head of every man . . . and God is the head of Christ" (1 Corinthians 11:3). By making us part of Himself, Christ has opened a way to bring all who are part of Him into obedience to the Father.

In 2012, a company called GE Aviation, part of the large company General Electric, acquired Morris Technologies, a supplier that specialized in additive manufacturing. GE wanted Morris's equipment and the expertise of Morris employees so that it could develop parts for jet engines. After the acquisition, GE completely revamped Morris's operations, wrapping up obligations to outside customers and refocusing the company on GE's aerospace goals. By making Morris Technologies part of its company, GE was able to direct all of Morris's work. We find the same idea with Jesus. By making us one with Himself, He is now able to direct us just as GE is able to direct Morris Technologies.[10]

Clue 4: The Reward for Participation

The fourth clue is the reward for participation. The reward for entering the kingdom is the same as the reward for enter-

---

10. Peter Zelinski, "Why Did GE Aviation Acquire Morris Technologies?" *Modern Machine Shop*, Jan. 2, 2013, http://www .mmsonline.com/columns/why-did-ge-aviation-acquire -morris-technologies.

ing the body of Christ. A rich young man once approached Jesus and asked, " 'Good teacher, what good thing must I do to inherit eternal life?' " (Matthew 19:16). Jesus described the conditions, including a plan to deal with the man's covetousness. The man became sad and went away, because he had a lot of money. He did not want to comply with the requirements. And then Jesus told His disciples, " 'Truly I say to you, it is hard for a rich man to enter the kingdom of heaven' " (verse 23). Note that the place this man was seeking to enter, into eternal life, was associated with the kingdom of heaven. Eternal life is the reward for entering the kingdom of heaven.

With the body of Christ, it is the same. Jesus described Himself as the door for the sheep. He said, " 'I am the door; if anyone enters through Me, he will be saved, and will go in and out and find pasture. The thief comes only to steal and kill and destroy; I came that they may have life, and have it abundantly' " (John 10:9, 10). Therefore we see that by entering into Jesus' body, by becoming part of Him—He Himself is the door—we enter into abundant life, the same eternal life that He talked about to the rich young man. The reward for entering the kingdom is eternal life; likewise the reward for entering the body of Christ is eternal life.

If a man tells you, "Hey, I just got a diploma," you know that he spent some time in school and then graduated. If a woman tells you, "Hey, I got a paycheck," you know that she did some work. If I tell you, "I got a speeding ticket," then you know that I was breaking the law. Based on the reward, we can guess the circumstances that led to that reward. And it is the same with the kingdom of God and with the body. The reward is the same, which indicates that the circumstances that led to that reward are also the same. Here is yet another clue that the kingdom of God and the body of Christ are identical.

Clue 5: Persecution

The fifth clue is the persecution that those who are members will encounter. Paul encouraged his fellow believers to continue in the faith, saying, " 'Through many tribulations, we must enter the kingdom of God' " (Acts 14:22). The tribulations he referred to were persecution. People encounter many persecutions when they set their hearts to enter the kingdom of God. The same is true of the body of Christ. Jesus said,

> "If the world hates you, you know that it has hated Me before it hated you. If you were of the world, the world would love its own; but because you are not of the world, but I chose you out of the world, because of this the world hates you. . . . All these things they will do to you for My name's sake, because they do not know the One who sent Me" (John 15:18, 19, 21).

Note that Jesus said these persecutions come for "My name's sake." When we enter into unity with Jesus, we become one with Him, and then we can be justly called by His name. We enter into His name. As we have studied, Jesus prayed to the Father, "Keep them in Your name, the name which You have given Me" (John 17:11). His name is not a phrase we add to our prayers or our conversations. His name is a state of being. Because of this name, this oneness with Christ, we encounter persecution.

A few years ago I was in the grocery store and was walking down the aisle with all of the snacks. Do you ever get cravings for something new? If you are like me, you tend to eat the same things day in and day out, and sometimes you just want some variety. There in the snack aisle I noticed a can of wasabi peanuts. Wasabi was something I had never tried before, so I put the can into the shopping cart. At home I opened it up and popped one of those peanuts into my mouth. Now wasabi, as I later learned, is a relative of the horseradish—very hot, and with a distinct taste. Some people love it; they even consider it a delicacy. I consider it horrible. Amy and I have a scale on which we rate foods from 1 to 10, 10 being one of the best things you have ever eaten, and 1 being the worst. In my opinion, wasabi peanuts were a scale re-arranger. The first peanut was the only one out of the entire can that got eaten.

Some colleagues and I went on a business trip to Indianapolis, and our team stopped in at a sushi restaurant for lunch. I had never eaten sushi before, but I was up for trying something new. When the plate arrived, the little sushi rolls were neatly arranged, and beside them was a green dipping sauce. It looked like it might be guacamole. I dipped one of the rolls in the sauce and took a bite. Immediately my tongue was on fire and a horrible but familiar flavor filled my mouth, just as when I ate the peanut. Again, it was the unmistakable taste of wasabi. Just as that burning, horrible taste was of wasabi both times I experienced it, so it is with the persecutions we encounter in the kingdom of God and in the body of Christ. The persecutions are the same in either case, another clue that the two messages are one and the same.

Clue 6: Jesus' Mission

The sixth clue is Jesus' mission. One time, the people of a certain region tried to keep Jesus from leaving them, but He replied, " 'I must preach the kingdom of God to the other cities also, for I was sent for this purpose' " (Luke 4:43). This is the foundational purpose for which Jesus was sent: to preach the kingdom of God far and wide.

When Jesus testified before Pilate, Pilate asked him, " 'So you are a king?' Jesus answered, 'You say correctly that I am a king. For this I have been born, and for this I have come into the world, to testify to the truth' " (John 18:37). Here we see that Jesus' foundational purpose was to testify to the truth. As we observed earlier, the book of John starts out, "In the beginning was the Word, and the Word was with God, and the Word was God" (John 1:1). This title for Jesus, "the Word," indicates that He is embodied in a set of teachings. John goes on, "But as many as received Him, to them gave He power to become the sons of God, even to them that believe on His name [the Word]" (verse 14). It is this oneness with Christ that we have been studying. Jesus came to preach the kingdom; likewise Jesus came to testify to the truth—to build up His body. The mission for the kingdom and the body are one and the same.

In my last year of college I took a machine design class. Toward the end of the semester the professor brought in a box of Tinker Toys, which are plastic parts that, fitted together according to a design, make simple structures. He divided the class into two groups and described a competition in which each team was supposed to build the tallest structure they possibly could. According to his rules, each team had a budget, and each of the Tinker Toys pieces cost a certain amount. To create the design we had to be conscious of the cost. My team came up with what we thought was a good design, and we figured up a list of parts based on how much our budget could afford. When our time was up, we handed our list to the teacher and told him how many of the hubs and blue dowels and red dowels we wanted. He and his assistant went behind the podium and began filling bags with parts.

The podium was big and solid, and they were hiding behind it, snickering and laughing. Finally they said, "OK, here are your parts." They brought out bags of parts, but the parts were not what we had ordered.

We told him, "Hey, this is not right. You messed up our order."

He said, "No. You ordered hubs, blue parts, and red parts. These may not appear exactly like the other parts you looked at, but I would call them hubs, and the other parts are blue and red." We thought we had ordered hubs that were thin and with eight holes around the circumference, but the hubs he supplied were tall, with only two holes. The blue and red parts we received were short instead of the long ones we thought we were getting.

The professor said, "These parts meet the specifications you gave me. But I will share a few more rules. You now have a budget for exchanging parts. The new budget is half of your original budget, and when you exchange parts, the new ones will cost four times more than what you paid for the original ones. You can get some other parts if you really need them."

There were choruses of, "Not fair! Not fair!" from the two teams, but the professor smiled. He was trying to teach us the important lesson that in engineering, parts must be ordered based on the characteristics that matter. If it is important that the part is ten inches long and a quarter inch in diameter, then those dimensions had better be specified on the order. If two different parts meet those specifications, then for engineering purposes they are considered to be the same. In the case of the Tinker Toys, the parts we received were different from the true specifications we needed; therefore we considered them to be different parts.

Now suppose we had ordered a part that was ten inches long and a quarter-inch in diameter, and the one we thought we were getting was red, but the one we actually got was yellow. Would we care? No, because it would not affect the specifications that mattered. Or suppose we ordered one that we assumed was wood and we received one that was plastic. Would we care? No, as long as it worked the same way. If parts meet the critical specifications, then the parts are considered to be the same. Likewise, there are two ways of describing Jesus' mission. One way is to describe it as the kingdom of God. Another way to describe it is as unity with Him. The essential specifications of both are the same, even though they look different at first glance.

Clue 7: The Final Message

The seventh clue that the gospel of the kingdom and the message of unity with Christ are one and the same is that they are both the final message to go to the world. At the beginning of this chapter we read the text about the gospel of the kingdom going to the entire world as a witness to them, and then the end will come. But there is more to the story. When John documented the Revelation that Jesus gave him, he wrote, "In the days of the voice of the seventh angel, when he is about to sound, then the mystery of God is finished, as He preached to His servants the prophets" (Revelation 10:7). You may remember that as each of the seven trumpets in Revelation sounds, another event in history unfolds. When the seventh and final trumpet sounds, Jesus comes back and the kingdom of this world becomes the kingdom of our Lord and of His Christ. It is the end of the world as we know it.

Just before that event, the text we just read says that "the mystery of God is finished." What is this "mystery of God"? Paul spelled it out clearly, writing,

> Of this church I was made a minister according to the stewardship from God bestowed on me for your benefit, so that I might fully carry out the preaching of the word of God, that is, the mystery which has been hidden from the past ages and generations, but has now been manifested to His saints, to whom God willed to make known what is the riches of the glory of this mystery among the Gentiles, which is Christ in you, the hope of glory" (Colossians 1:25–27).

So the mystery of God is Christ in you. That mystery will be completed just before Jesus comes again. The gospel of the kingdom must go to the whole world, and then the end will come; likewise, this mystery of God will be completed just before the end comes. These are two different ways of looking at the same thing.

Putting all of the clues together, the kingdom and the body are similar in the following ways. Both of them

- have the same entrance requirements
- are located in our hearts
- have the same authority structure
- have the same reward for participation
- have the side effect of persecution
- are referred to as the purpose for which Jesus came
- have messages closely tied with the end of the world

Based on these clues, I believe it is clear beyond any reasonable doubt that the kingdom of God and the body of Christ are one and the same. This gospel of the kingdom has not gone to the whole world as a witness to its inhabitants primarily because a large segment of Christians are proclaiming an incomplete message. When we understand the details about the body of Christ and how those details clarify the message of the kingdom, the necessity of an attitude of obedience comes into sharp focus. This expanded detail I believe will enable us to fully preach the gospel of the kingdom.

What, then, should we do? I suggest three steps: study, apply, and share. First we need to study the Bible again to make sure that we adequately understand this message of unity with Christ. Second, we need to apply in our lives the message of unity with Christ. This message is not a theoretical one but an eminently practical one—one in which we wholeheartedly seek out and act on the will of God, depending on Him for strength. Third, we should share this message with those around us.

The Rest of the Story

Paul Harvey was known for a radio program called *The Rest of the Story*. In college I would go out to my truck during breaks and tune in to the broadcast. In that radio program he would describe some obscure fact or little-known event that had happened, and he would withhold the person's name until the very end. Then at the end, he would reveal who he was talking about, and usually it was a famous person. And then he would say, "And now you know *the rest of the story*."

In this chapter we have studied the gospel of the kingdom and we have studied the body of Christ. These two messages are one and the same, describing a unity with God where he dwells in us through the Holy Spirit, enabling us to do what is right and making us part of Himself. Let's reevaluate our message and ensure that we are clearly sharing the gospel of the kingdom, a kingdom in which the subjects of the kingdom are subject to the king. Let's share the whole message, including the opportunity to become part of God's Son through internalizing His words. Let's share the rest of the story.

Discussion Questions:

1. What is the message that must go to the whole world before the end comes?

2. List some of the evidence that the kingdom of God and the message of unity with God are one and the same.

3. Explain the two dangerous errors described in this chapter that destroy the very heart of the gospel.

4. Summarize some implications of the idea that the gospel of the kingdom and the message of unity with Christ are the same.

5. Come up with your own verbal image to illustrate the "kingdom of God."

6. Imagine you are a teacher. Write a test question designed to evaluate your students' understanding of the material found in this chapter.

7. According to the first angel of Revelation 14, what is the eternal gospel? The Scriptures cannot be broken, so both the first angel's message and the passages about God's grace must influence our understanding of the gospel (see Romans 3:28, Galatians 2:16, Philippians 3:9). How do we harmonize these texts that may at first seem contradictory?

8. What are some of the problems of considering these two messages in isolation from one another?

9. Try brainstorming some additional attributes or features of the body of Christ beyond those listed as clues in this chapter. Do all of them find a counterpart in the kingdom of God, or are some of them unique to the message about unity with Christ? Explain.

10. When you combine the message of unity with God and the gospel of the kingdom, how does it affect your understanding of the latter?

11. If the gospel of the kingdom must be preached to the whole world, and then the end will come, and if the gospel of the kingdom is the same as the message of unity with God, what importance does this place on the message of unity with God? Is there anything in your life that needs to change to adjust for this information?

12. See how many of the following clues you need in order to guess which individual they refer to:

▸ He was born in Kentucky and grew up in Indiana.

▶ He was known for his strict honesty.

▶ He was elected to public office.

▶ He was accountable to the entire American people.

▶ He had a mission to keep the United States from splitting over the issue of slavery.

▶ He spoke at the dedication of the National Cemetery at Gettysburg.

▶ He was assassinated on April 15, 1865.

▶ A likeness of his head is carved into Mount Rushmore.

It only takes a few clues to definitively identify this man. How many of the clues listed in this chapter does it take for you to definitively identify that the gospel of the kingdom is the message of unity with Christ? Which ones do you believe are most conclusive, and why?

CHAPTER SEVEN

A Mighty Helper

One summer during my college years I taught sailing at a camp in Alabama. Occasionally in my free time, I took one of the sailboats out and enjoyed some sailing myself. Alabama is not known for its good sailing weather, but one afternoon a big thunderstorm blew through to the south of the camp. Though far enough away that all the lightning and the rain were beyond us, we still got the wind from it. The lake was whipped into whitecaps, and the waves were about three feet tall. A friend and I decided to take one of the boats out. We took our chances with the lightning—I would not recommend it, but we did it. As soon as we exited the cove where the camp was located and entered the main channel of the lake, the wind whipping over the surface of the lake filled the sail and accelerated that boat like I had never before experienced. In fact, it was pushing us so hard that the hull of the boat began hydroplaning across the surface of the water. That day we learned what sailing is really all about.

Suppose we had dipped our hands over the side of the boat and tried to paddle along. Would it have helped any? No. If anything, it might have hindered us. Instead, we focused on setting the sail. Then the power of the wind carried us along. In our Christian experience, it is the same. We have a choice to make. We have to set the sail, so to speak, but God then works in us to give us the power to do what He wants us to do. When we decide to do God's will, God works mightily to help us carry out that decision. And that is the focus of our next study.

The Three Elijahs' Messages

This concept is shared in three very special messages in the Bible, what I would call the three Elijahs' messages. We are familiar with the first Elijah, the one who prayed on Mount Carmel, and fire came down from heaven and consumed his sacrifice. But then there is a prophecy in the book of Malachi that says, "Behold, I am going to send you Elijah the prophet before the coming of the great and terrible day of the Lord" (Malachi 4:5).

Jesus indicated that this prophecy has two fulfillments. When the disciples asked Him about it, He said, " 'Elijah is coming and will restore all things' " (Matthew 17:11). Jesus here indicated that at that time, part of the prophecy was still in the future. And then He added, " 'But I say to you that Elijah already came, and they did not recognize him, but did to him whatever they wished. So also the Son of Man is going to suffer at their hands.' Then the disciples understood that He had spoken to them about John the Baptist" (verses 12, 13). Therefore John the Baptist was a fulfillment of that prophecy in Malachi. He was what we could call the second Elijah. But as Jesus said, there is still an Elijah to come, who will also fulfill the prophecy in Malachi. This future fulfillment is the third Elijah.

These three Elijahs all have the same message. All three preach a message of repentance for restoration to God. By studying the content of the first two Elijahs' messages, we can learn much about the third message that is prophesied to go forth just before Jesus comes again.

One time at the place where I work, the company launched a new disc replacement for spine surgery. When we launched the product, the marketing team used multiple avenues to get the message out. They distributed brochures, they conducted cadaver labs to train the physicians, and they trained the sales reps to discuss the product with the clinicians and hospital administrators. The form of publicity was different for each of these efforts, but the message was always the same. All were trying to describe the benefits and risks of the product and convince the physicians to give it a try. In the same way, with the Elijah messages, the content is the same, even though the form is different in the three messages.

The First Elijah—A Message of Repentance

The first Elijah preached a message of repentance for restoration to God. King Ahab had gone way off the deep end into idolatry, so Elijah came to Ahab with a message from God: " 'As the LORD, the God of Israel lives, before whom I stand, surely there shall be neither dew nor rain these years, except by my word' " (1 Kings 17:1). Then Elijah turned around and fled. He disappeared for the next three and a half years.

At the end of that time, he came back to King Ahab. When Ahab saw him coming, he said, " 'Is this you, you troubler of Israel?' " (1 Kings 18:17).

Elijah replied, " 'I have not troubled Israel, but you and your father's house have, because you have forsaken the commandments of the LORD and you have followed the Baals' " (verse 18). Shortly afterward on Mount Carmel, Elijah prayed before the people gathered there,

"O LORD, the God of Abraham, Isaac and Israel, today let it be known that You are God in Israel and that I am Your servant and I have done all these things at Your word. Answer me, O LORD, answer me, that this people may know that You, O LORD, are God, and that You have turned their heart back again" (verses 36, 37).

First, Elijah indicated that trouble had come upon Israel because the people had transgressed the commandments of the Lord. And then in his prayer on Mount Carmel he indicated that he was working together with God to turn the hearts of the people back to God. That is the Elijah message—a message of repentance for restoration to God.

The Second Elijah—Also a Message of Repentance

The second Elijah preached a message of repentance for restoration to God, just as did the first Elijah. You may remember when Zechariah, John the Baptist's father, was in the temple, and Gabriel came to him, announcing that John the Baptist was going to be born, even though Zechariah and his wife were very old. He told Zechariah what the ministry of John was going to be like, saying, " 'He will turn many of the sons of Israel back to the Lord their God' " (Luke 1:16). Gabriel added, " 'It is he who will go as a forerunner before Him in the spirit and power of Elijah' " (verse 17). The angel directly quoted the prophecy in Malachi. Here is the original: "Behold, I am going to send you Elijah the prophet before the coming of the great and terrible day of the LORD. He will restore the hearts of the fathers to their children and the hearts of the children to their fathers, so that I will not come and smite the land with a curse" (Malachi 4:5, 6).

Gabriel made a substitute for one of the clauses in the prophecy. Instead of "and the hearts of the children to their fathers," he said, "and the disobedient to the attitude of the righteous." Those two phrases are synonymous, however. The way the hearts of the children are turned back to their heavenly Father is by turning them from disobedience to righteousness.

Some years ago a speaker had a ministry focused on restoring and building up families, which is certainly a good ministry. One time he said that his ministry was the message of Elijah because he was restoring the hearts of the children to their fathers. But the prophecy of Elijah indicates that the one speaking will turn the hearts of the children to their *heavenly* Father, as the first Elijah did—he turned the people's hearts back to their heavenly Father. And this is what John the Baptist, the second Elijah, did too. Therefore we can expect that the third Elijah will turn the hearts of the children back to their heavenly Father.

The Third Elijah—Clues from the First Two Elijahs

Our quest is to understand the full content of the third Elijah's message and the significance it has for us in our day. John the Baptist gave an amazing clue about that. The Jewish leaders had sent people to John to ask him, "Who are you?"

John replied, " 'I am a voice of one crying in the wilderness, "Make straight the way of the Lord," as Isaiah the prophet said' " (John 1:22, 23). Here John the Baptist, the second Elijah, linked his message to the prophecy in Isaiah. We have already seen evidence that the content of the three Elijahs' messages is the same, and therefore we can expect that the prophecy in Isaiah that John the Baptist applied to himself also holds as a description of the third Elijah's message.

The prophecy in Isaiah from which John quoted says,

A voice is calling, "Clear the way for the Lord in the wilderness; make smooth in the desert a highway for our God. Let every valley be lifted up, and every mountain and hill be made low; and let the rough ground become a plain, and the rugged terrain a broad valley; then the glory of the Lord will be revealed, and all flesh will see it together; for the mouth of the LORD has spoken" (Isaiah 40:3–5).

This call is to remove those things that hinder God from working and to build up those areas that are lacking.

The place where I work requires yearly performance reviews. In the review form, one section asks several questions, including, "What does this employee need to start doing in order to better meet the mission?" The next question on the form asks, "What does this employee need to stop doing that is hindering him or her from meeting the mission?" The intent behind the form is to get people to regularly evaluate what they need to stop doing or start doing in order to more effectively align their work with the direction of the company.

That idea has actually been around for quite a while, at least since the time of Isaiah, because that is what Isaiah was saying in this prophecy. Let every mountain be removed, let every valley be filled up in order to make a highway for the Lord. We are to remove some things—to stop doing the things in our lives that are preventing Him from working in our hearts. We are to add some things—to start doing those things in our lives that will enable God to work more effectively in our hearts.

One of the Longest Prophecies in the Bible

This passage in Isaiah is actually part of a much bigger prophecy. Isaiah chapter 40 through 66 is one long, twenty-seven-chapter prophecy. Sometimes we do not zoom out enough to really understand the full impact of what such a passage is saying.

One time I went backpacking in the Linville Gorge in North Carolina. About two thousand feet deep, its large rock walls soar hundreds of feet high on either side of the gorge, and down in the bottom flows the Linville River, with big waterfalls and rapids. Sections of the gorge have immense old-growth poplar and hemlock trees, some of which are four or five feet in diameter. Our intended course was to enter the gorge near the upper end, hike nine miles down the river, and then catch a trail that exited up a narrow ridge that split its way through the cliff line. The ridge offered a thin window between the towering cliffs where one could hike out of the gorge without resorting to technical rock climbing.

The Linville Gorge is a wilderness area, and the trails are not marked. In the upper part of the gorge, which is more traveled, the trails are easy to follow. But in the lower part of the gorge, the main trail becomes faint and splits into multiple crisscrossing footpaths. To make matters worse, several hikers have attempted to mark the trail with survey tape, and their interpretations of the correct trail differed. Some of the survey marks appear to be missing, so some leads extend for a distance but then abruptly end. The route-finding is very confusing and difficult. After some searching, we eventually found the trail that extended up the ridgeline to exit the gorge. The trail was steep, about three-quarters of a mile, with sections at a thirty-degree incline. It was like climbing a two-hundred-story building with a forty-pound backpack. We arrived at the top just as the sun was making its descent to the western horizon.

In the parking area we found a fifteen-passenger van. A couple of people were sitting in the van, and they looked troubled. One of them, a woman, was crying. We asked her if we could help, and she explained that they were part of a college outdoor program. The program had organized a backpacking trip for students, most of whom were camping in the wilderness for their first time. The people in the van were supposed to pick up the backpacking party and shuttle them back to their cars at the other end of the trail. Unfortunately the party had become lost down in the gorge. Already they had spent an extra night down there, and time was running out before they would spend a second extra night. If those backpackers could have risen above the trees and seen where they were, then they could have seen the whole picture and located the ridge line and the trail out of the gorge.

When we are studying Isaiah 40 through 66, it is much like that. Amazing passages are found there, but unless we zoom out enough to see that all of these passages are part of the same train of thought, we will miss the beauty of what the passage is really saying. Let's zoom out and look at the historical context for Isaiah 40 through 66.

Retracing the Steps from Babylon to Jerusalem

The people of Israel disobeyed God and were taken captive to Babylon. God eventually called them to come out of Babylon. Those who were willing returned to Jerusalem, which was desolate and wasted. There they rebuilt the temple and restored worship of the true God. Though it is a historical reality, it is also prophetic of future events. Isaiah 40 through 66 is about this whole process of the Israelites getting carried to Babylon, coming out of Babylon, going back to Jerusalem, and restoring the worship of God. Look at the clues from this passage:

▸ Transgressions resulted in the Israelites departing from Jerusalem to Babylon (Isaiah 50:1).

▸ They came into subjection to Babylon (Isaiah 47:6).

▸ God's people were called out of Babylon (Isaiah 48:20, 21).

▸ Babylon was the origin of the journey (Isaiah 52:11).

▸ God led the people through the wilderness (Isaiah 49:8–11).

▸ The way of the Lord leads to Jerusalem (Isaiah 49:14–18).

▸ The redeemed come to Jerusalem (Isaiah 51:11; 60:4).

▸ Jerusalem will be filled with the redeemed (Isaiah 54).

▸ God's ultimate goal that He's working toward is to fill Zion with those who are righteous (Isaiah 60:21).

We'll find it helpful to define a couple of symbols. The first is *Jerusalem*, which was the city around which God's true system of worship revolved. The temple was there. All the yearly feasts were held there. No other altar to God existed than the one in Jerusalem. Since the whole true worship of God centered in this city, Isaiah uses Jerusalem as a symbol for the worship of the true God.

Then there is *Babylon*. Babylon was the capital city of the empire to which the people of God were carried when they disobeyed. Babylon was full of slavery, idolatry, and evil spiritual influences. Isaiah uses Babylon as a symbol of the system of false religion that God's people find themselves in when they disobey. In the heart of this passage is a call for God's people to come out of Babylon and return to Jerusalem.

If we are to understand the full implications of this passage in Isaiah, it is important for us to understand that it is one prophecy, even though it is many chapters long. Multiple themes weave through the passage like willow shoots in a basket, tying all of these chapters into one entity. One of those themes is comfort for Jerusalem. This starts in Isaiah 40:1–2 and reappears many times through the passage, all the way to Isaiah 66:13. A second theme is Babylon, which runs through the central chapters of the prophecy. A third theme is a "highway" for God, and it is this theme that holds a particularly encouraging message for you and me. It is the Elijah message.

The Central Theme

This theme starts with the passage we have already read, Isaiah 40:3–5, the one from which John quoted. This call is a high one, to bring our lives into conformance with God's will.

The theme resurfaces in the next chapter of Isaiah.

"Do not fear, you worm Jacob, you men of Israel; I will help you," declares the LORD, "and your Redeemer is the Holy One of Israel. Behold, I have made you a new, sharp threshing sledge with double edges; you will thresh the mountains [those mountains that we read about that had to be made low] and pulverize them, and will make the hills like chaff. You will winnow them, and the wind will carry them away, and the storm will scatter them; but you will rejoice in the LORD, you will glory in the Holy One of Israel" (Isaiah 41:14–16).

One time I went to New York City on a business trip. The plane was on the approach to La Guardia Airport, and my seatmate motioned to me and said, "Hey, if you look, you can see the Freedom Tower." I saw it rising from the site where the two World Trade Center buildings used to stand. Including its antenna, the Freedom Tower is 1,776 feet tall, symbolic of the year that the Declaration of Independence was signed. The Tower stands right where there used to be a mountain of rubbish from those first two World Trade Center buildings. Now, in your mind's eye, imagine standing at the foot of that mountain of rubbish. As you look at the towering heap, a tiny movement catches your attention. You look closer and see an inchworm crawling up one of the beams. If that worm were to set its mind to clear the rubbish, would it succeed? No, it could not even begin. It took mighty cranes, huge machines, backhoes, and months of work, and then the mountain was moved.

The people of Israel were facing a similar circumstance. Jerusalem had been turned into a pile of rubbish, and they were being called back to restore it. The text in Isaiah says, "Do not fear, you worm Jacob." Though our strength is that of worms, God is our helper in this effort. He will help us carry out the work of reform, removing every sin that hinders, and adding in new actions that are His will. God is the one who makes us capable of rebuilding spiritual Jerusalem, of coming back to the right way of worshiping Him. He is the one who helps us repent. The decision is ours, but the power is His.

The Passion of God

The theme of "the way for the Lord" carries on in the next chapter of Isaiah. There he wrote, "The Lord will go forth like a warrior, He will arouse His zeal like a man of war. He will utter a shout, yes, He will raise a war cry. He will prevail against His enemies" (42:13).

Isaiah then starts quoting God: " 'I have kept silent for a long time, I have kept still and restrained Myself. Now like a woman in labor I will groan, I will both gasp and pant' " (verse 14). That sounds pretty serious, right? If God is standing up and gasping and panting out of His zeal and passion, stay out of His way! At least that may be our first impression. But then God reveals the purpose for all of this passion. He says, " 'I will lay waste the mountains and hills and wither all their vegetation' " (verse 15a). God is the one laying waste the mountains that stand between us and the restoration of that true worship of God.

He continues, "I will make the rivers into coastlands and dry up the ponds" (verse 15b). Remember when the children of Israel came up to the Jordan at flood stage, when they were on the border of Canaan? God stopped up the water of the Jordan, mighty as the flow was, and the people crossed over. And that is what He is talking about in Isaiah. Our God is going to do monumental things to prepare the way for His people to restore true worship. God concludes, " 'I will lead the blind by a way they do not know, in paths they do not know I will guide them. I will make darkness into light before them and rugged places into plains. These are the things I will do, and I will not leave them undone' " (verse 16).

When it comes to preparing the way for the Lord, do you feel like a blind person working on a construction crew? Do you feel as though you are sitting on one of those big roller machines, tasked with the responsibility of paving the road, and you cannot see? In other words, do you not have the ability to do what God is asking you to do? Do not fear, because God says that He will lead the blind by ways they do not know. He will guide them. He will make the rough places smooth before them. We have a decision to make, but the power to accomplish it is His.

In the spring of 1977, a young man named Rick heard about a five-mile benefit run for a lacrosse player who had been paralyzed in an accident. He told his father Dick about the opportunity and asked his father if he would run it with him. His father agreed. However, Rick has cerebral palsy. He is confined to a wheelchair. His father pushed him in that wheelchair the five miles of the race. They came in second-to-last, but they finished.

After that race, Rick told his father, "Dad, when I'm running, it feels like I'm not handicapped." Rick's father had always wanted as normal a life as possible for his son. So he began taking him out on additional races. They have run more than a thousand races together. They have completed marathons and duathlons and triathlons. In all of these races, never once did any of the power come from Rick. It all came from his father. Dick would either push his son in the wheelchair or, for the swimming component of the triathlon, he would put Rick in a raft, and pull the raft along behind him. For the bicycle portion, he would put Rick on a special seat, and Dick would be the one pedaling for his son.[11] All the power came

---

11. Team Hoyt, "About Team Hoyt," http://www.teamhoyt.com/About-Team-Hoyt.html.

from the father. None of the power came from Rick himself. He had a decision to make. He asked his dad to help him, but his dad was the one who actually made it happen.

In our spiritual walk, it is the same. When we come to God, and He tells us the things He wants us to do, we do not have the ability to do it, any more than Rick had the ability to do that five-mile race. But the power does not come from us; it comes from God. We only give that initial consent. We determine to go in the direction God wants us to go, and then God makes it happen.

Beware of the Crooked Paths

Isaiah not only talks about straight paths; he reveals that some have chosen crooked paths. He speaks of the wicked, saying,

> Their feet run to evil, and they hasten to shed innocent blood; their thoughts are thoughts of iniquity, devastation and destruction are in their highways. They do not know the way of peace, and there is no justice in their tracks; they have made their paths crooked (Isaiah 59:7, 8).

God wants us to make the path straight and smooth, but those who persist in going their own ways are making crooked paths. They are doing the opposite of what God wants.

Isaiah says, "Who is among you that fears the LORD, that obeys the voice of His servant, that walks in darkness and has no light? Let him trust in the name of the LORD and rely on his God" (Isaiah 50:10). Sometimes when we follow God's ways, it seems as though we are walking in darkness. We may not understand His reasons, and His commands may not make intuitive sense, but God's message to us is, "Follow anyway."

Those who insist on a way that seems more sensible are

on dangerous ground. God's message to them is, " 'Behold, all you who kindle a fire, who encircle yourselves with fire brands, walk in the light of your fire and among the brands you have set ablaze" (Isaiah 50:11a). Those who are not content to follow God's ways want to find a "better" way, so they look for a path of their own. What is God's warning? " 'This you will have from my hand. You will lie down in torment' " (verse 11b). When God tells us to go one direction and we decide, "No, I think I have a better way," and we go off in our own direction, we put ourselves in great danger.

When the United States Supreme Court ruled in favor of same-sex marriage, a lot of people rejoiced at the news. These view acceptance of the homosexual lifestyle as progress. However, they are choosing a way that is contrary to the clearly expressed will of God. While we should always love those who struggle with homosexuality, and we should treat them kindly and with respect, at the same time, the Bible is very clear that those who participate in those activities and refuse to repent will not inherit the kingdom of God. To choose our own way when God has thoroughly defined His way is serious business.

When my family was living in California, we went camping at Mount Lassen National Park. Mount Lassen itself is a volcano, and the park has several other volcanoes and many volcanic features. We visited one of the hydrothermal fields where there were boiling mud pots and steaming fumaroles. The Park Service has installed boardwalks and walkways in the area, and there are numerous danger signs that warn visitors, "Mud pots and steam vents are very hot. Ground is soft. Serious burns have occurred. Stay on trails and boardwalks." We were very careful to stay on the safe areas and held our children's hands tightly. Right near the trails you could see the bubbling mud pots and the steam wafting out of the hillsides and smell the sulfurous fumes from deep down in the earth.

Lassen is a very interesting, odd place. We had a safe time, though, because we stayed on the trail.

Around the same time that we visited the park, a woman walking by the Sulfur Works, one of the hydrothermal features at Mount Lassen, decided to step off the trail onto an area that appeared to be solid ground. It was only a crust of mud about an inch thick, and her foot broke through the mud and plunged into the boiling, acidic water below. To try to save her foot, she had to be airlifted to a hospital. She had disobeyed the instructions. She stepped off the safe way onto ground that she thought was solid but was not. She paid an extremely painful and damaging price for her mistake.

In the same way, we should stay in the way that God has defined and not make for ourselves crooked paths of our own choosing that are contrary to His revealed will.

A Mighty Helper

God gave clear instructions regarding how to prepare the way. Through Isaiah He said,

> "Build up, build up, prepare the way, remove every obstacle out of the way of My people. For thus says the high and exalted One who lives forever, whose name is Holy, 'I dwell on a high and holy place, and also with the contrite and lowly of spirit in order to revive the spirit of the lowly and to revive the heart of the contrite' " (Isaiah 57:14, 15).

How are we to prepare the way for the Lord to come? God declares, "A Redeemer will come to Zion, and to those who turn from transgression in Jacob" (Isaiah 59:20). The way to God is prepared when we turn from transgression. That means forsaking our former ways and thoughts. Then God abundantly pardons us.

Isaiah 57 continues with God's declaration, saying,

"For I will not contend forever, nor will I always be angry; for the spirit would grow faint before Me, and the breath of those whom I have made. Because of the iniquity of his unjust gain I was angry and struck him; I hid my face and was angry, and he went on turning away, in the way of his heart. I have seen his ways, but I will heal him; I will lead him and restore comfort to him and to his mourners, creating the praise of the lips. Peace, peace to him who is far and to him who is near . . . and I will heal him" (16–19).

Oh, how precious God is, that He would understand our frailty and help us! What thanks is due Him for dealing tenderly with us, restoring us to His image in spite of the corruption He has to wade through in us to get the job done. To me, it is so touching that God looks on us in our predicament and has mercy. He does not require that we be perfect in order to approach Him. He does not require that we clean ourselves up before we come to Him. Oh, the graciousness of the Lord, who has not left us to try to find our way back to Him! All he requires is a decision, and a weightless one at that, to follow Him. He then provides the power for us to carry out that decision. He receives us as we are and begins working in us to help us fully conform to His will. We raise the sail, but He comes as a mighty wind and fills that sail, carrying us where He wants us to go.

We have nothing to offer. We cannot give to God our affections. We cannot bring an offering of righteousness, only vile corruption. But God knows how to turn corrupt people into pure people. We do not need to make it to Jerusalem before God receives us. He receives us at Babylon and helps us get to Jerusalem.

On the morning of February 21, 1963, a two-year-old boy named Leslie was walking with his father. They came upon an old oil drum mostly embedded in the ground. Leslie playfully jumped on top of the strange object, but with a clang the loose cover shifted, and he plunged fifteen feet into an abandoned cesspool that was full of nauseating gases and dangerously little oxygen. The boy sank to his waist in the deep muck at the bottom. The frantic father tried to reach his son, but he could not fit through the foot-wide opening. Emergency personnel soon arrived, but they also were too large to fit. They feared that if they lowered lines to the boy and tried to pull him up, he might lose his grip and fall face-down into the muck and suffocate. If they dug a way into the cesspool with bulldozers it might collapse. If they did not work quickly, he could be overcome by the lack of oxygen.

Kenneth Magallanes stood nearby with his mother, watching the emergency unfold. He quietly told her, "I can fit through that hole, Mama." His mother hesitated a moment, but then she thought of Leslie, terrified and crying. "OK, you can try," she told her eleven-year-old son. When he informed the rescuers of his wish to help, one of them warned Kenneth that the cesspool gas could kill him. "I still want to go," he replied.

The fire chief at first refused, but he feared that a delay might be fatal to Leslie. Reluctantly he changed his mind. Fire fighters tied a rope sling around Kenneth and lowered him into the cesspool. He sank to his knees in the muck, but he located Leslie, wrapped his arms around him, and the rescuers pulled the two of them up. Almost at the top, they could not both fit through the hole. Kenneth tried to hand Leslie to a fireman, but he began to choke with nausea, and Leslie slipped from his grasp. The firefighters pulled Kenneth up for fresh air. He revived and asked to go down again. This time the rescue workers gave him a second rope to secure around Leslie, then lowered Kenneth again. He secured the rope around Leslie, and the rescuers pulled both of them to safety.[12]

---

12. Theodore Schuchat, "He Went Into the Old Cesspool to Save a Young Child's Life," *The Spartanburg Herald*, Sept. 1, 1971, https://news.google.com/newspapers?nid=1876&dat=19710901 &id=hX4sAAAAIBAJ&sjid=98wEAAAAIBAJ&pg=7319,16413 &hl=e

We are like Leslie. We have landed in a terrible predicament. When Leslie was sunk in the muck, powerless to rescue himself, Kenneth stepped in. He did not wait for Leslie to free himself. He did not wait for Leslie to clean himself up. Kenneth slipped down into the cesspool in spite of the stench, difficulty, and danger to himself, and he came to Leslie's rescue. That is what God does for us. He sees our predicament, steps into our corruption, wades through our mess, and frees us if we are willing.

Come Out of Babylon

The Israelites were carried from Jerusalem to Babylon. Then those who remained in Jerusalem rebelled again. So Nebuchadnezzar captured the city again, and deported almost all the remaining Israelites to Babylon. A few of the very poorest people remained in Israel, but for all practical purposes, everybody was taken to Babylon. This figure applies to us. Just as virtually all of the Israelites ended up in Babylon, virtually all of God's true church has ended up in Babylon. We all have become corrupt. We all have sinned and fall short of the glory of God. All have become an unclean thing. But God is ready to work with us.

There are two classes of people in Babylon: wicked people who are willing to change, and wicked people who are not willing to change. God works with the wicked people who are willing to change, and He helps them return to Jerusalem, figuratively speaking, and restore the worship of the true God. On the other hand, those not willing to change are left in Babylon, and they will be destroyed when God renders judgment on Babylon.

In the spring of 1980, Mount St. Helens began to have minor eruptions along with earthquakes of increasing frequency. A bulge formed on the north slope of the mountain, expanding five feet per day. Volcanologists gave dire warnings about an impending massive eruption. Sheriff's deputies announced mandatory evacuation orders. Many heeded the warnings and fled to safety. However, some refused to flee, including Harry R. Truman, a salty old character who ran a lodge at Spirit Lake and had lived on the mountain for more than fifty years. The authorities barred access to the mountain, but in a response to them laced with profanity, Harry declared, "Block the ____ road, and don't let anyone through till Christmas ten years ago. I'm havin' a ____ time livin' my life alone. I'm king of all I survey, I got ____ plenty whiskey, I got food enough for 15 years, and I'm settin' high on the ____ hog."[13]

One week later, on May 18, an earthquake shook the mountain, causing the northern slope to buckle and collapse. A thunderous boom shattered the morning calm as the mountainside exploded in a gigantic lateral eruption. An avalanche of debris swooped down the mountainside at up to 150 miles per hour. It struck Spirit Lake, sending a six-hundred-foot-high wave smashing into a ridge on the north side of the lake. Harry's lodge was buried under 150 feet of volcanic debris. His body was never recovered.[14]

Similar to the residents near Mount St. Helens, we have been warned to flee from Babylon. Let us not be satisfied with our current position, taking comfort that things have always been this way and remain pleasant. Rather, let us embrace change and flee from the impending destruction. Let us set our hearts on returning to Jerusalem, trusting that God will open the way as we step forward in faith to restore His true worship in our lives.

In this chapter we have studied the three Elijahs' messages,

---

13. Rowe Findley, "Mountain with a Death Wish," *National Geographic*, January 1981, http://ngm.nationalgeographic.com /print/1981/01/mount-st-helens/findley-text.

14. Stephen L. Harris, *Fire Mountains of the West* (Missoula, MT: Mountain Press Publishing, 2005).

especially the third one that prepares the way for the Lord to come again. Like the first two messages, the third message is one of repentance. It emphasizes the importance of making a decision to follow Christ. We have also concluded that we have no power to carry it out, but that the power comes from Christ.

Maybe you need to make a commitment to Christ today, or recommit your life, or reaffirm your commitment. Whatever your background, will you choose today to follow Christ with all your heart? Will you make a decision to surrender every area of your life to Him, and depend on Him to give you the strength to alter your ways to line up with His will? Let's make every mountain low and fill in every valley in our hearts to prepare the way for the Lord.

Discussion Questions:

1. Who are the three Elijahs?

2. What is the key message that the Elijahs give?

3. Summarize the evidence that the content of the three Elijahs' messages is essentially the same.

4. Describe one of the themes that runs through Isaiah 40–66 which shows that the passage is one continuous thought.

5. What is the significance of the three Elijahs' messages being the same?

6. How is the third Elijah's message related to the end of the world?

7. Compare the attributes of the people of Jerusalem just before Nebuchadnezzar carried them to Babylon and the characteristics of Christians in our day. How are

they similar? How are they different?

8. What are some mountains you see standing between you and restoring the true worship of God? What about some valleys?

9. If you combine the information about the three Elijahs with what you have learned about the kingdom of God, what implications arise?

10. How can we improve our reliance on God's ability to help us make every mountain low and build every valley up?

11. What do you think about humans' role versus God's role in restoring the true worship of God?

12. Weigh the evidence that Isaiah 40–66 is all part of the same thought. What other implications do you see? Which of those implications is most important?

CHAPTER EIGHT

Taking the Kingdom By Force

One time I was assigned to a team tasked with revamping an important test method. The test was intended to imitate the performance of a product in a blood vessel. The test method results were notoriously variable, sometimes shifting by a factor of ten from one test run to the next. Numerous efforts had been conducted over the years to improve the performance, all to no avail. Our team developed a plan to isolate the root cause, and after a long process of elimination, all fingers pointed at the mock vessel. Upon closer inspection, we could see mold release from the manufacturing process on the inside of the component. We theorized that this mold release was gradually being wiped off during use, causing the frictional properties to change, thus affecting the results. After a thorough scrubbing, the mock vessel was reinstalled, and immediately the test results stabilized. We were thrilled and promptly presented the data to the rest of the department, claiming victory in the effort.

Unfortunately, when we conducted a large series of tests to validate the cleaned vessel, the updated system failed the test. We were terribly disappointed. Some immediate variability may have been resolved, but there was still long-term variability present. Six months of work by a ten-person team had not resolved the issue. Over the next eighteen months, the team finally determined that the polyurethane from which the mock vessel was made degraded over time. They replaced the mock vessel with a different material and reran the validation testing. This time the system passed with excellent performance. The changes in the original mock vessel could not be seen with the eye. Only through a long process of careful testing could enough be understood about the system to make a good engineering decision.

One of my engineering instructors once declared, "Most of reality is invisible. That is why I love mechanical engineering. You can take two pieces of metal that look exactly the same on the outside but they have different properties. And if you understand the different properties of those materials, then you can use that knowledge to your advantage and create systems that actually work." What he said about mechanical engineering, and reality in general, was true. And not only is it true in the physical realm but also in the spiritual realm. Most of reality is invisible.

One of those invisible realities is the reality of God's authority. Throughout this book we have studied the all-important attitude. Based on the love in our hearts for God, we must adopt an attitude of seeking and doing God's will, depending on Him for strength to carry it out. We have talked in some depth about the first part, how it is imperative that we seek to know and do God's will. But that is just half of the equation. The other half is that we must depend on God for strength in order to actually make that decision a reality in our lives. And that is faith—what it takes to enter the kingdom of God.

A Violent Faith

Jesus talked about a violent kind of faith. He said, " 'The Law and the Prophets were proclaimed until John; since that time the gospel of the kingdom of God has been preached, and everyone is forcing his way into it' " (Luke 16:16). At another time Jesus expressed the same idea in even more descriptive terms. He said, " 'From the days of John the Baptist until now the kingdom of heaven suffers violence, and violent men take it by force' " (Matthew 11:12). So this entering into the kingdom of heaven is described as people pressing into it. The pressing is so strong that it could even be described as violent.

One time Amy and I needed a new washer and dryer. I saw a Black Friday ad in a catalog where they were selling a nice washer and dryer set for half off the list price. On a big-ticket item, that was a lot of money, so I got up early on Black Friday and drove down to the department store a little over an hour from where we lived. By the time I arrived at four o'clock in the morning, already a line of people stretched from the front door down the sidewalk almost to the end of the building. By the time the store opened about six, the line was past the end of the building all the way out almost to the street. When they finally opened the doors, the people pressed in to the store to get whatever item it was that they had their heart set on. The scene was almost like a stampede. And it is that kind of pressing, that kind of aggressive pursuit of God, that we need to have in our Christian experience.

If I could sum up the idea in one sentence, it would be this: we should exercise a strong faith in God's authority, so strong, in fact, that it could be termed "violent." Not that we are violent toward one another but that we are violent—we are super aggressive—in our pursuit of God.

Jacob set an example of this super-aggressive faith. He had a twin brother named Esau. Typically, twins get along well, but not so with Jacob and Esau. Things got so bad between them that Esau intended to kill Jacob. Jacob got wind of it, and he fled to some of his mother's relatives in Haran.

Along the way, Jacob stopped at a place called Luz and lay

down to get some sleep. He took a stone and used it as a pillow—a miserable situation. As he was trying to sleep, he started to dream. In his dream he saw a ladder that stretched from earth to heaven, and the angels of God were ascending and descending on that ladder. God was at the top of the ladder, and He spoke to Jacob. He passed on to him the promise that He had given to Abraham and Isaac:

> Thy seed shall be as the dust of the earth, and thou shalt spread abroad to the west, and to the east, and to the north, and to the south: and in thee and in thy seed shall all the families of the earth be blessed (Genesis 28:14, KJV).

Then God went on to promise that He would be with Jacob, saying,

> Behold, I am with thee, and will keep thee in all places whither thou goest, and will bring thee again into this land; for I will not leave thee, until I have done that which I have spoken to thee of (verse 15, KJV).

Jacob got up the next morning, amazed and afraid, and said, " 'Surely the LORD is in this place, and I did not know it' " (verse 16). He took the rock that he had used for a pillow and set it up as a pillar, a memorial to God. He anointed it with some oil and made a vow to God and said, " 'If God will be with me and will keep me on this journey that I take, and will give me food to eat and garments to wear, and I return to my father's house in safety, then the LORD will be my God'" (verses 20, 21).

Jacob journeyed on from there to Haran, where he spent the next twenty years. He got married, had children, and became wealthy. Then God commanded him, "Return to the land of your fathers and to your relatives, and I will be with you" (Genesis 31:3). Jacob began making preparations, and God spoke to him a second time, urging him, "I am the God of

Bethel, where you anointed a pillar, where you made a vow to Me; now arise, leave this land, and return to the land of your birth" (verse 13). Note that Jacob was not basing his decision to return to Canaan on his own feelings. As much as he might have wanted to return to Canaan, he was basing his decision on God's command. Jacob was exercising faith.

A Definition of Faith

What is faith? When we ask this question, we often turn to Hebrews 11:1: "Faith is the assurance of things hoped for, the conviction of things not seen." But that vague definition is difficult to apply in a concrete manner in our lives. We do learn from it that faith has to do with invisible realities. Faith is the way we interact with these unseen realities. But if we were to boil down the definition of faith to its very basic elements and come up with a definition that we could apply, what would it be?

I spent some time wrestling with this concept, and here is my working definition: "Faith is submitting to God's authority and relying on it, even when doing so is not intuitive." Here is an example: the centurion (the one whose servant was healed) called Jesus "Lord," and he was so sure of Christ's authority that he was willing for Jesus to just speak the word and heal his servant from a distance. Likewise, the Canaanite woman pressed Jesus to heal her daughter, even ascribing to herself the position of a dog under the master's table. Blind Bartimaeus called loudly and repeatedly for Jesus and then ascribed to him the position of "Rabboni," or master. These all submitted in faith to Jesus' authority and relied upon it.

How does having faith mean submitting to God's authority? A king rules over a kingdom. We often think of a kingdom as a piece of land, but kings make laws for people. It is the subjects of the kingdom over which a king rules. In order to become subjects of the heavenly kingdom, we must be subject to the heavenly king. Submitting to God's authority is the first part of faith.

The second part of faith is that we must rely on His authority even when it is not intuitive to do so. Jacob exercised both of these elements of faith. God commanded him, "Return to the land of your fathers," and Jacob obeyed. He *submitted* himself to God's authority. But he also *relied* on God's authority. God had promised that He would be with Jacob wherever he went, that He would bless him and bring him back to the land of his fathers. Many dangers beset his way, yet Jacob set out anyway, relying on God's promise of protection.

The Test of Faith

When Jacob neared Canaan, he sent messengers on ahead to let Esau know that he was coming. Jacob desired to smooth things over as much as possible. However, the messengers returned and said, "Esau is coming to meet you, and four hundred men are with him." What Esau's intent was is clear—he was going to make good on the threat he had made twenty years earlier to kill Jacob.

Jacob was highly troubled. God had told him, "Return to the land of your fathers," but he now faced a terrible dilemma. He could go forward and face what seemed like certain death, or he could flee, but doing so would be to disobey God's command.

Rather than flee, Jacob took his problem to God. He fervently prayed, his deep emotion resonating through the written record:

"O God of my father Abraham and God of my father Isaac, O LORD, who said to me, 'Return to your country and to your relatives, and I will prosper you,' I am unworthy of all the lovingkindness and of all the faithfulness which You have shown to Your servant; for with my staff only I crossed this Jordan, and now I have become two companies. Deliver me, I pray, from the hand of my brother, from the hand of Esau; for I fear him, that he will come and attack me and the mothers with the children. For You said, 'I will surely prosper you and make your descendants as the sand of the sea, which is too great to be numbered' " (Genesis 32:9–12).

Jacob set his heart to keep going in the direction God had directed him to go, even though it made no human sense.

A friend of mine is a pilot. He has a two-seater airplane that he built, and he installed a number of good instruments in it. Suppose that night falls and fog rolls in while he is on one of his flights. And suppose he feels that he is flying level and as if he knows where his plane is located and which direction he is headed. However, when he looks down at his instruments, and they tell him something different from his feelings, he will surrender his feelings and fly based on what those instruments say. At least, he had better do that, because a pilot can get completely disoriented when visibility goes away. He could be flying upside down and not even realize it. In such situations, a pilot has to surrender his feelings and follow what the instruments say. We, in our lives, also have to surrender our feelings and follow God's will instead of what we want when the two disagree with one another.

The Ugly Beautiful and the Beautiful Ugly

Jacob got up the next morning and made preparations to meet Esau. He gathered a number of gifts and sent them on ahead of him. Then on the second night, he again went and prayed. The Bible does not record exactly what he said that second night, but I am sure it was the same sentiment in his heart that he had the first night, asking God to protect him from Esau.

The Bible says, "Then Jacob was left alone, and a man wrestled with him until daybreak" (Genesis 32:24). Jacob again knelt in prayer, but suddenly a hand gripped him like a vice. The thought probably flashed through Jacob's mind, *This is one of Esau's men! He has indeed attacked!* But God had told him to go to the land of Canaan, and Jacob was set on obeying. Instead of running, he began to struggle with his assailant. He did not give up, but rather he exerted every ounce of energy to follow what God had told him to do.

When it comes to our feelings, often the way to life seems like the way to death, and the way to death seems like the way to life.

When I was growing up, we lived for a few years in western North Carolina. The North Carolina Department of Transportation had hydroseeding trucks, and at times they would put in a wildflower mix and spray the seeds all over the roadsides. Later, when the plants sprang up and began blooming, the roadsides turned gorgeous everywhere. Now imagine with me the men who were operating that hydroseeding truck. Their supervisors did not send them out to the pretty roadsides. They sent them out to the ugly roadsides, the ones where construction had been completed, or that were experiencing erosion. Mile after mile, every job the men went to was ugly. So before them are barren roadsides, but behind them springs up beauty wherever they have been.

So it is in the Christian life. When we set our heart to follow God, sometimes the future looks bleak, at least in this life. We think, "Wow, I will have to give up things that are meaningful to me and give up pleasures that I hold dear. Following God is going to cost me." But as we follow God, we look back to where we have been, and we see beauty springing forth at every turn. When we sow righteousness, then joy, hope, and peace are the result. Who can measure the worth of a clear conscience? Who can put a price on having peace in one's heart? Going forward, the Christian experience at times looks ugly, but looking back, it is pure beauty.

The North Carolina Department of Transportation also had mowers. From time to time they would mow the roadsides in order to keep the vegetation down. Imagine you are riding on one of those large mowers. The roadsides are beautiful, covered in wildflowers. Everywhere you look, it is gorgeous. But you glance behind your mower, and as far as you can see, there is only stubble. So it is when we follow our own will. The future looks rosy, beautiful, and full of promise for fun and pleasure. But after following our own ways for a while, when we look back on our history, ruin and destruction mark those ways.

Wrestling in Pain

Jacob was at one of those points in his life when he was wrestling with the decision to follow God or flee. And he was wrestling with his assailant. When the assailant saw that he had not prevailed against Jacob, he touched Jacob's hip and dislocated it. That searing pain would utterly discourage most people. Jacob was in a wrestling match for his life, and such a move by his assailant left no doubt as to who had the greater strength. There was no way Jacob could win in this physical struggle, at least not to human sight.

But at this moment, Jacob saw an opportunity. That painful touch from his assailant revealed to Jacob that he was not struggling with one of Esau's men but with a supernatural being. He probably began reasoning in his mind, "It was in the context of prayer that this guy came upon me. Could it be that this is God?" Suddenly Jacob went from defense to offense. He began fighting his assailant to pin him down. Sometimes when we wrestle with God, it hurts, but we must keep on striving anyway, not forgetting the opportunity that comes in that wrestling match.

On March 15, 1910, a team of people was drilling for oil in California's San Joaquin Valley. On that day they hit oil. The pressure of that oil was so great that it blew the drilling equipment back up out of the hole and formed a column of oil 200 feet high and 20 feet in diameter. This strike became known as the Lakeview Gusher #1, the largest in the oil industry's history. It ruined the drilling equipment and eventually destroyed the derrick that was used to drill the hole. It buried the control house as well. However, in the space of four hours, the workers laid two and a half miles of pipeline. Soon after that, they built dikes and dams to hold in the oil. As the oil erupted out of the ground, they funneled it into a lake and then piped it down to some storage containers, and eventually out to the coast of California. So much oil was coming out of that one well that it brought world oil prices down by 70 percent. At peak flow it was spilling out 125,000 barrels of oil per day. Altogether the owners recovered about 4.5 million barrels of oil from that well as it flowed for 544 days. The day when the oil first erupted, the workers lost their drilling equipment. However, none of them were sad about it—it was apparent to all what they had gained.[15]

A Hidden Golden Opportunity

Jacob experienced loss that night when his assailant dislocated his hip. But, though it was terribly painful and debilitating, Jacob saw his opportunity. How many of us would love to hear from God? Wouldn't you love to hear God's voice? If God is asking you to give something up in your life, do not get too focused on the pain of what you have to give up. If God is asking you to give something up, who then is talking to you? God is. What an amazing opportunity! Jacob saw that opportunity, and he seized it.

---

15. Michael S. Clark, "The Lakeview Gusher," San Joaquin Valley Geology, last updated Oct. 10, 2015, http://www.sjvgeology.org /history/lakeview.html.

Finally his assailant said, " 'Let me go, for the dawn is breaking' " (Genesis 32:26). I love those words, "Let me go." They are spoken by the one who dislocated Jacob's hip with a mere touch. Such a one could have extricated himself from Jacob's grasp at any time. Instead he utters an almost plaintive plea, "Let me go."

Most people would welcome the opportunity for their assailant to leave, but not Jacob. When we are wrestling with God, He allows Himself to be caught by the grasp of faith. When we surrender to God's authority and rely on it, He allows Himself to be caught by us.

I was about eight years old when my family began getting mysterious calls. The phone would ring, we would pick it up, and the line was dead. Or we would pick up the phone and you could tell someone was on the other end, breathing into the receiver, but they were not saying anything. This happened numerous times.

One day we came home and the door was standing open. Our house had been broken into, and the thieves had stolen many valuable things. It turned out that all those phone calls were made by the thieves, checking out when we were home. Once they had figured out our schedule, they came when we were not there, and they robbed us. In the carport, a brand new riding lawnmower was still there. My parents said to themselves, "Those thieves must have seen the riding mower. They will surely be back."

Some days later, my mom and I were at home alone when the phone rang. Both of us were occupied, and we missed the phone call. Soon afterward a black Ford Bronco pulled into the driveway pulling a U-Haul trailer. We were renting a house on a 300-acre ranch, and the house sat about five hundred feet from the road. When the vehicle got to our house, the driver pulled right off the end of the driveway and drove around in the grass behind the house. I began screaming, "The robbers are here! The robbers are here!"

My mom was already on the phone with the police. She firmly told me, "Sh-h-h . . . be quiet!" One of the robbers got out. He walked around to the front of the house and banged on the door. My mom said to the robber, "What do you want?"

The man replied, "Is Russell there?" Russell is the name of my brother. My mom replied, "Russell who?" The robber gave the name of one of our neighbors down the road, who had also been robbed a few days before.

My mom said, "No, he doesn't live here." The man got back in the Bronco and sped off.

A minute or two later, a police car came careening up to the driveway. My mom said to the dispatcher, "The robbers are no longer here. They turned left out of the driveway. Have the officer follow them." The police continued the chase, and they eventually pulled the men over and arrested them.

When those thieves left, I was filled with relief, knowing that they were not going to break down the door and hurt us. And when I saw the police car at the end of the driveway, I was even more relieved. "The law is on our side. They are going to save us from these evil people." That reaction is natural for people when they are being assailed—they are relieved to see the assailant go away.

But not so with Jacob.

Going Where God Wants

When Jacob's assailant offered to leave, Jacob hung on even more, and in words that will live forever he replied, " 'I will not let you go unless you bless me' " (Genesis 32:26). Here Jacob displayed violent faith. This is what it means to take the kingdom of heaven by force. When we know that God has given us a command to follow and we cannot muster the strength to obey, we hang on to God, saying, "I will not let you go unless you bless me." Jacob was not asking for material blessings but for God to fulfill the promise He had already given him. God had said, "I am with you and will keep you wherever you go, and will bring you back to this land."

A man named Mike shared with me his battle against pornography. One time he was at home alone, and the desire to view forbidden websites washed over him with immense power. All sorts of rationalizations poured through his mind. But the very specific command of God is, "Thou shall not commit adultery." And to look on a woman to lust after her is to commit adultery with her in your heart. He knew there was no getting around that. He knew the command of God.

I do not know what his exact words were in that moment, but the sentiment of his prayer was, "I will not let You go unless You bless me." He was wrestling, fighting against the temptation. On the one hand was his desire; on the other hand was God's will. He hung on to God, and God gave him the victory that day and in many days to follow. Mike is now a leader in his community. He helps many other people figure out God's will for their lives and follow it. He exercised the spirit that Jacob exercised: "I will not let you go unless you bless me."

Israel and His Like-Minded Descendants

Jacob's assailant said to him, " 'What is your name?' " (Genesis 32:27).

He replied, "Jacob." Jacob means deceiver, and it is a name that he had lived up to all too well. He had deceived his father and stolen his brother Esau's blessing. And he had cheated his brother Esau in a very unfair transaction, trading a bowl of lentils for his brother's entire birthright. It had to be with a touch of shame that he said, "My name is Jacob."

His attacker said to him, " 'Your name shall no longer be Jacob, but Israel; for you have striven with God and with men and have prevailed' " (verse 28). Israel means "he strives with God." From "Israel" we get the word *Israelite*. The Israelite nation is biologically descended from Israel, but those who are true members of Israel are those who have the spirit that Israel had. Paul wrote,

> He is not a Jew who is one outwardly, nor is circumcision that which is outward in the flesh. But he is a Jew who is one inwardly; and circumcision is that which is of the heart, by the Spirit, not by the letter; and his praise is not from men, but from God (Romans 2:28, 29).

The burning question is, are we willing to part with our own ways in order to follow God's ways? Are we willing to submit ourselves to His authority and to depend on Him wholeheartedly to help us obey? This is what it means to press our way into the kingdom, to take the kingdom of heaven by force.

Jacob then turned the question back on his assailant and said, " 'Please tell me your name' " (Genesis 32:29). In typical humble fashion, God did not press home what Jacob already knew. Instead He simply responded, "Why is it that you ask my name?" And God blessed him. Jacob named that place Peniel, which means "the face of God." He said, " 'I have seen God face to face, yet my life has been preserved' " (verse 30). Jacob knew who it was that he had been striving with—none other than God Himself.

I used to work in lawn care, and one of the crew members was named Max. We got to know one another fairly well driving between jobs, and we started talking about spiritual things. One day, he confided in me, saying, "I am really struggling with a prescription pill addiction."

I told him, "Max, if you make up your mind to do what is right and you muster all of your strength and determine in your heart that you are going to follow God, you will fail, if that is as far as you go. You must depend on a strength outside of what you naturally possess. If you depend on your own strength, you are done for. But if you depend on God, asking Him for His strength, He will give you the victory."

We pulled up to the job site, and as we were preparing to step out of the truck, Max said, "I have pills in my pocket right now, and I am really struggling with taking them. I could take them and you would not even know." It was clear that Max was engaged in some serious spiritual warfare. Would he choose God's way even though it felt like the wrong way? Every desire in him was screaming, "Take the pills!"

I told him, "Max, pray like we talked about. Do not depend on your own strength. Depend on God. And I will be praying for you too." The lawn took us a couple of hours to mow, and all the while I was pouring out my heart to God. "OK, God, I have told Max how to depend on You. Please come through for him."

We completed the job and were loading up the equipment on the trailer. Max had a beautiful smile on his face. He pointed to some white powder on the asphalt and said, "I prayed like you told me to, and God gave me the strength. I crushed my pills." Max exhibited the two elements of true faith. He chose to follow God's ways, and he depended on God to help him get the victory. He was exercising the spirit of Israel.

We have discussed the need for a super-aggressive faith and that we should have a faith in God so strong that it could even be termed violent. So what about you? Is there a place in your life you are struggling to surrender fully even though you know God's will? Maybe it is a drug addiction such as my coworker Max struggled with. Maybe it is pornography as Mike struggled with. Maybe it is an intemperate lifestyle. I do not know what battle you are fighting. But if you recognize something in your life that is not in accordance with God's will, there is hope. You do not have to depend on yourself to muster up the strength to overcome. We must depend on God for His strength. God needs our decision, but we must have His strength. Will you exercise the spirit of Israel that says, "I will not let you go unless you bless me"? I hope that is your desire. Let us take the kingdom of heaven by force.

Discussion Questions:

1. What is the definition of faith given in this chapter?

2. When Jacob heard that Esau was coming against him with four hundred men, why did Jacob not flee?

3. What does it mean to have "violent" faith?

4. What does it look like for a person in our day to wrestle with God?

5. This chapter discussed the importance of a mighty faith but did not look in depth at where that faith comes from. Discuss how a person can increase his faith.

6. Recount a time in your own life when surrendering your will to God was a struggle. How do you feel about the outcome now?

7. What is the relationship between faith and the all-important attitude described in chapter 1?

8. Refute the idea that a strong faith is simply a solid confidence that God will grant a person eternal life.

9. Describe some other people in the Bible who displayed a "violent" faith.

10. Elaborate on the idea of a time of "Jacob's trouble" as described in Jeremiah 30:7. What is the significance of it for us today?

11. Compare and contrast the experience of Jacob and Esau. How are they similar? How are they different?

12. Evaluate the statement, "When it comes to our feelings, often the way to life seems like the way to death, and the way to death seems like the way to life."

CHAPTER NINE

How to Know God's Will

The night of July 9, 1943, the Allies landed 170,000 men on the beaches of Sicily. The amphibious landing was supposed to be followed by two waves of paratroopers, the first with 2,200 men, and the second with 2,000 more. As the invasion got underway, Major General Matthew Ridgway, who was responsible for the airdrop, realized that the second wave of paratroopers was not needed, so he tried to call it off. By that time there was so much momentum that it was not practical to stop it, but the hesitation did delay the drop by one night.

Unfortunately, the message did not make it down through the chain of command from the Air Force to the Navy to the gunners that the drop had been delayed. The next day the amphibious landing continued, but German dive-bombers attacked the ships, and the American anti-aircraft gunners were all on edge. On the night of July 11, the second wave of paratroopers swooped in over the drop zone in formations of nine transport planes at a time. The first two formations successfully dropped their men, but as the third formation flew through, a nervous American gunner opened fire. As soon as he opened fire, other gunners on the beach and on nearby ships also opened fire. The ensuing mêlée caused massive damage to the fleet of aircraft dropping the men. Twenty-three of the 144 planes were shot down. Of the ones not shot down, many were badly damaged. One plane landed back at base with a thousand holes in the fuselage. Eighty-three soldiers were killed and another 235 were wounded. It was the worst friendly-fire incident up to that point in United States history.

During the subsequent investigation, one of the gunners said, "We had no idea. It never crossed our minds that we were firing on Allied aircraft."[16] That night as they wildly shot into the dark sky, the gunners exerted everything within their power to fend off what they perceived to be the enemy, all the while fighting against the very power they professed to be serving.

You and I are at risk of making a similar mistake. It is possible for us to be fully convinced that we are doing God's will while at the same time directly opposing Him. Jesus talked about this danger. In a prophecy of things to come, He said, " 'They will make you outcasts from the synagogue, but an hour is coming for everyone who kills you to think that he is offering service to God' " (John 16:2). Notice that it is not atheists whom Jesus predicted would do the persecuting; it is people who think they are serving God. These professed servants will actually be fighting against Him. They will fall into the trap of which Solomon warned, "There is a way which seems right to a man, but its end is the way of death" (Proverbs 14:12).

Since it is possible to think we are serving God and at the same time serve Satan, how can we avoid this disaster? How can we know that we are truly doing what God wants? I wish I could offer a concise formula in which we could plug certain

---

16. Robert F. Dorr, "Friendly Fire's Deadliest Day," *America in WWII*, http://www.americainwwii.com/articles/friendly-fires-deadliest -day/.

inputs and, on the far end, get an exact knowledge of God's will. It is not that easy, but we are not left in the dark either.

In this chapter I will share the best method I know for maximizing our chances of discerning God's will. The method can be summed up in one sentence: "Gather the evidence." Several major sources of information are available regarding God's will, and we need to gather the evidence from as many of those sources as possible. Once we have the evidence, we can draw a conclusion about what is God's will.

I will review five sources: (1) the Bible; (2) nature; (3) godly counselors; (4) circumstances; and (5) our conscience. Each of these sources has its strengths and weaknesses, so gathering the evidence from multiple sources increases the chance of accurately determining God's will.

Source 1: The Bible

The first source of evidence is the Bible, the very clearest source of God's will. Its strength comes from being the most authoritative of the five sources. Paul wrote, "All Scripture is inspired by God and profitable for teaching, for reproof, for correction, for training in righteousness; so that the man of God may be adequate, equipped for every good work" (2 Timothy 3:16, 17). Note the authority: the Scriptures are inspired by God.

From time to time I like to take prayer walks. I used to find a quiet spot in the woods behind our house, kneel down, and tell God, "I want to hear Your voice, Your personal voice regarding my specific situation. Will You please speak to me audibly as You did with the prophets of old?" I never heard anything. Once in a while I still pray that way. However, one day the realization dawned that if I were to hear an audible voice, I would still have to verify it. Such a voice could be God speaking to me, or, God forbid, it could be a demon. It could be an angel, or it could be a chemical imbalance in my brain. Whatever I heard, I would still have to compare it to some standard and confirm that it was authentic.

But what would that standard be? The very best standard is the Scriptures. If the Scriptures are the standard, then is it not right to view them as the audible voice of God to us? If anything, they are better than the audible voice of God.

In a medical device manufacturing environment, parts are inspected before they are shipped. A gauge pin or block used in inspection must be several times more accurate than the parts being measured by it. When it comes to spiritual truth, the Bible is the standard. It is much clearer than other sources.

The Scriptures can be considered more accurate than the audible voice of God because their authenticity is confirmed by the prophecies. The prophecies are evidence that the Scriptures did not originate in someone's imagination but came from God Himself. Peter wrote, "We have the prophetic word made more sure, to which you do well to pay attention as to a lamp shining in a dark place" (2 Peter 1:19). Because they have proven true, the prophecies in the Bible provide a foundation upon which to base our belief. Consider how specific some of the prophecies of the Messiah are. He was to:

- ▶ be born of a virgin (Isaiah 7:14)
- ▶ be born in Bethlehem (Micah 5:2)
- ▶ be a descendant of David (2 Samuel 7:14–16)
- ▶ be called out of Egypt (Hosea 11:1)
- ▶ be full of miraculous powers to heal (Isaiah 35:4–6)
- ▶ come riding on a donkey (Zechariah 9:9)
- ▶ be betrayed by a close friend (Psalm 41:9; Psalm 55:12, 13)
- ▶ be sold for thirty pieces of silver, which would be

thrown to the potter in the temple (Zechariah 11:12, 13)

All of these very specific prophecies happened exactly as they were foretold.

A number of the messianic prophecies have multiple predictions within one prophecy. For example, Isaiah 52 and 53 says that God's special servant would:

▶ have His appearance heavily marred (Isaiah 52:14)

▶ be despised and rejected (Isaiah 53:3)

▶ be silent when accused (Isaiah 53:7)

▶ be numbered with the transgressors (Isaiah 53:12)

▶ die (Isaiah 53:9)

▶ pay the penalty for the sins of others (Isaiah 53:5, 10–12)

▶ have a grave with the rich (Isaiah 53:9)

▶ live, even though He died (Isaiah 53:10)

One of these predictions happening as predicted might leave room for doubt as to whether that event had happened by chance. However, the probability of these multiple predictions being fulfilled by chance becomes exceedingly small.

Not only are the prophecies very specific and some have multiple predictions in one prophecy, many of them accurately predicted events hundreds or even thousands of years into the future. Some went against contemporary trends. Still others are time-bound, giving specific timeframes for their fulfillment. A very worthwhile study is to investigate the great prophecies contained in Daniel, Isaiah, Revelation, and elsewhere in the Scriptures.

These characteristics give confidence that the prophecies had more than just a mere human origin. If God gave predictions that accurately came to pass, we gain confidence that His predictions which have not yet come to pass will happen. And if God can accurately tell the future, which is a very difficult thing to do, then we gain confidence that He can accurately describe what happened in the past, including an accurate account of Creation and an accurate account of the war between good and evil that broke out in heaven.

Furthermore, His record in prophecy gives confidence that those areas of the Bible that are not prophetic are accurate as well. For example, a prophet might have given predictions about the future that came true, but he might also have given much non-prophetic counsel about things relating to God's will for our lives. Because of the credibility built through the prophecies, we have confidence that the other things the prophet said were also true. This train of logic based on the prophecies gives us a strong foundation upon which to base our belief.

I have often marveled to myself, "Where would I be without the anchor of prophecy?" If I did not have these prophecies that give strong evidence that the Bible is true, I would be awash in a sea of ideas. But we have a durable anchor. These predictions that were beyond human ability provide a strong confirmation that the Bible has a supernatural origin.

The strength of the Bible is that it is the most authoritative source for truth. The weakness of the Bible (not that there is a weakness in its truth) is that at its most fundamental level, the Bible is black ink on white paper. People who do not know the Bible may see no immediate value in it. A friend of mine grew up as an atheist in China. She said that as a young person she viewed the Bible in the same way as Greek mythology. To her it was just fanciful tales. I believe she had that experience because there is no relational aspect to mere words on a page. Not until she had the opportunity to interact with Christians did she begin to seriously consider the claims of the Bible, and finally she gave her life to Christ.

The second challenge with the Bible is that it is like a puzzle. Someone once told a friend of mine, "I read the Bible once. I know what it says. I do not need to read it anymore." That attitude is like taking a jigsaw puzzle, dumping it out on a table, turning the pieces right side up and saying, "I have seen the puzzle. There is no need to look at it anymore." But once we have all the pieces out on the table, we need to start putting them together, piece by piece, until the picture emerges. So it is with the Bible. We can read it from cover to cover, but that is just the start. Then we need to put text with text, passage with passage until we see the deep, beautiful meanings buried in it. Somebody who has only read the Bible once or twice may fail to grasp the deep gems of truth that emerge after more thorough study.

Source 2: Nature

The second source for gathering evidence about God's will is nature. Paul wrote, "Since the creation of the world His invisible attributes, His eternal power and divine nature, have been clearly seen, being understood through what has been made, so that they are without excuse" (Romans 1:20). Nature reveals complex design that gives strong evidence of a master designer, indicating the character of the Creator and teaching lessons about His will. The power required to ignite a star, the gentleness that inspired a peaceful mountain valley, the love behind the design of a rose or chickadee song or taste buds all reveal attributes of God's character.

Someone in the Brazilian jungle who has never read the Bible still has the testimony from nature. Even though they may have never heard the story of Creation from the first chapters of Genesis, yet by looking at the marvels of a fiery sunrise, the fine-tuned design of a flying bird, and the miracle of birth they can conclude, "Something big happened here."

A few years ago, I visited the Ford Rouge Complex in Detroit. The facility covers six hundred acres, and it is used to manufacture Ford F-150 trucks. Massive machinery forms the metal, and thousands of workers assemble the parts until at the end of the assembly line, out rolls a pickup truck. But God has made it so that humans have the ability within themselves to produce another human being. That is like creating a factory inside a Ford truck to make another Ford truck. It is a striking engineering marvel. Any who have attempted to design a mechanism will have an appreciation for how impossibly difficult it would be to make something like that. This kind of marvel cries out to us saying, "Something big happened here."

Nature encompasses more than just the wild places and natural settings. At its more fundamental level, nature as a source of truth can be viewed as "truth from secular sources." For instance, you could read the Bible from cover to cover and find only small tidbits of information about health. The information is good advice, but comparatively little appears in the Bible about the subject. However, millions of people the world over are studying what leads to the best health. Their research provides evidence regarding the laws of health. For example, a neurosurgeon would not look to the Bible to teach him how to help people recover their strength. He would discover truths about human anatomy and pathology by studying textbooks and journal articles, participating in fellowships, and discussing cases with peers. These non-biblical sources are deep sources of truth related to the laws of health. And the laws of health are, in a sense, a revelation of God's will, because He is the one who created us to operate that way. Those things may not be contained in the Bible, yet the laws in nature are still something from which we can gather information when trying to discern God's will.

The strength of nature is that it is available to everyone.

The challenge with nature is that it has been corrupted by sin. We see truth that has been confounded. For example, those who study the laws of health sometimes come up with poor conclusions. They may suggest fad diets, or medicines that are harmful, or lifestyles that are detrimental. We have to be discerning, knowing that nature is not the most authoritative source for truth.

Source 3: Godly Counselors

The third source for evidence of God's will is godly counselors. Paul wrote,

> He gave some as apostles, some as prophets, and some as evangelists, and some as pastors and teachers for the equipping of the saints for the work of service, to the building up of the body of Christ. . . . We are no longer to be children, tossed here and there by waves and carried about by every wind of doctrine . . . but speaking the truth in love, we are to grow up in all aspects into Him who is the head, even Christ (Ephesians 4:11, 12, 14, 15).

These apostles and teachers and preachers and others were specifically given abilities to help share God's will—they were to establish the church in sound doctrine. They were to speak the truth in love. They were to help share evidences of what He wants us to do.

Some years ago, Amy and I hit a rough patch in our marriage. Someone suggested a wonderful Christian counselor, so we went. The counselor worked with us, sharing different tools we could use to relate with one another in healthy ways, improve our communication, and negotiate conflict. Often it was uncomfortable, but he was sharing with us a knowledge of God's will. The truth greatly benefitted us then and continues to benefit us a decade later. To this day I am grateful for his input. It helped turn our marriage from one that was just barely moving along to one that is very deep and rich and meaningful. He was a source through which the evidence of God's will came.

Just as it was uncomfortable for us in the counseling sessions, we as humans have a tendency to dislike things that feel bad. If something hurts, we tend to push back or reject it. Because of this tendency, we need to be very careful that when someone gives us advice, we do not automatically oppose it, especially if that advice comes from a trustworthy persons and it goes against our natural desires. We need to tune in because it may very well be an opportunity to grow.

King Ahab of Israel and King Jehoshaphat of Judah met and laid war plans together. Before setting out to battle, King Jehoshaphat asked for a prophet of the Lord to give them counsel regarding the Lord's will. Ahab sent for Micaiah, but he added, " 'I hate him, because he does not prophesy good concerning me, but evil' " (1 Kings 22:8).

Micaiah arrived and told the two kings, " 'I saw all Israel scattered on the mountains, like sheep which have no shepherd. And the LORD said, "These have no master. Let each of them return to his house in peace" ' " (verse 17). King Ahab was infuriated, and he had Micaiah thrown into prison, telling the governor, " ' " 'Put this man in prison and feed him sparingly with bread and water until I return safely' " ' " (verse 27). King Ahab rejected the advice because he did not like it, and he proceeded to the battle, where he was slain.

In order to escape Ahab's folly, we should view rebuke as a gift. The psalmist wrote, "Let the righteous strike me; it shall be a kindness. And let him rebuke me; it shall be as excellent oil; let my head not refuse it" (Psalm 141:5, NKJV). And Solomon said, "The way of a fool is right in his own eyes, but a wise man is he who listens to counsel" (Proverbs 12:15). If you think you are right and somebody else is telling you that you are wrong, know that it is the fool who goes on steadfastly thinking he is right. The wise man will pay attention to that advice and see if there is not some good counsel in it. Another passage says it even more bluntly: "Do you see a man wise in his own eyes? There is more hope for a fool than for him" (Proverbs 26:12). We need to be very careful that we do not think our ideas are better than everybody else's.

Let me try to illustrate how easy it is to justify ourselves in our own minds. Think of someone you know who is wise in his or her own eyes. Picture that person in your mind's eye. Who is it—a co-worker, a friend, a spouse? When I was preparing this chapter, a person or two came to my mind. But that is the concerning point. How many of us pictured ourselves? It is altogether too easy to think of how other people need to change so they can draw closer to the truth. If we are to avoid playing the part of a fool, we have to view ourselves as the ones who need to apply this lesson.

Recently a man gave me advice that was hard to hear. He did not see the entire situation, and it seemed that the advice was unfair. But he is a godly man, and as I write this, I am listening with all ears and I am processing through it and trying to figure out how to best apply his advice. That process can be difficult, and probably none of us is perfect at it, but I would very much like to be a wise man. We can learn to take advice from other people, even if that advice comes across as contrary to what we want to hear. Let's be wise and seek for whatever truth may be in their counsel.

My family had a good laugh recently. For Christmas my parents gave me a keepsake folder of things they had collected throughout my childhood. It had little notes, prizes I had won, good attendance records and so forth. One of the items was a page of one hundred sentences, a punishment that my dad gave me when I was ten years old. All down the page was written, "I love my brother Russell. I love my brother Russell.

I love my brother Russell." I actually did not remember the punishment, but my dad said that when he gave me those sentences, it crushed me. According to him, at that time I would have preferred a spanking rather than that assignment. When I finished writing the sentences and turned them in to him, I included this note. "I would never want to take English from you because your assignments would be too long. It would surely take me a year to do one. I would die from exhaustion in half an hour. I wouldn't be around anymore." We had a good chuckle at my childish antic. At that age I had little awareness of the opportunity that comes from listening to advice. I hope I have grown over the years! We need to be very careful to listen when somebody gives us advice, especially a trustworthy person.

The strength of godly counselors is that they are relational. If a friend says to me, "Hey, check out this passage in the Bible; I think it applies to your situation," it will likely mean more to me than if I came across that passage on my own. Godly counselors are like a mirror. They can show us things in ourselves that are blind spots for us—things we would pass by and not even recognize.

The downside of godly counselors is that they can still be wrong. I read an article in which somebody was interviewing a famous Hollywood actor. He was talking about his upbringing and his childhood, and specifically his religious experience. He said his father was a devout Catholic, and he was also a Catholic. His reason was, "I know my father would never lie to me." It may be true that his father would never lie to him, but it is also possible for someone to be sincerely wrong. Think of all the mothers and fathers the world over who have different religious beliefs—Hindus, Buddhists, atheists, Christians, Jews. They cannot all be right. Therefore we need to be careful with human counselors and use their advice as only part of the evidence when determining God's will. Even though counselors many times give us good advice, we still need to test their advice against the standard—the Bible—and determine whether that advice truly is good or not.

A special case that falls under this heading is tradition. Traditions are customs and beliefs passed from one generation to the next. That transmission happens through counselors—parents or teachers or religious leaders. Tradition can be helpful for providing an initial framework of belief. My children chew with their mouths closed because they were told to. The only reason for it is that in our culture, doing so is good manners. That behavior has become a tradition, if you will. In many cases it would be unwise to entirely throw out our beliefs and start over with just the things we have a clear reason for. In this area, continual remodeling is better than wholesale reconstruction.

The moral framework provided by tradition is just a start, however. The problem with tradition is that if an error is ever introduced, that error can be propagated for generations without any good rationale for it. If errors compound, one can end up far from the truth. The Pharisees fell into this trap. They held tightly to their tradition, but that tradition had departed from the instructions God had given them. Jesus reprimanded them for it: " 'Why do you yourselves transgress the commandment of God for the sake of your tradition?' " (Matthew 15:3). Tradition should always yield to the higher authority of the Scriptures.

One winter afternoon my wife and I took our kids to Foster Falls in Tennessee. We pulled into the parking lot about half an hour before sunset, with just enough daylight to take a short walk to an overlook with a good view of the falls and the gorge. We were still in sight of the parking lot when a hiker approached and asked, "Is there another parking area nearby?" He described how he had set out to do a loop hike but now he could not find his car. I told him that this was the only parking area around. He pulled out a trail map, and we studied it together.

It soon became apparent that the man had parked at an entirely different trailhead. The loop hike he intended to do turned back after about four miles, but he missed the turnoff and hiked the entire length of the twelve-mile Fiery Gizzard Trail. Mile after mile he had hurried along the trail, never pulling out his map to check his location. He just continued on that trail because it kept leading forward. In so doing, he ended up a day's hike from his car. Thankfully for him, a relatively short shuttle ride brought him back to the other trailhead.

In our spiritual lives, the stakes are much higher. While there is nothing inherently wrong with tradition, it is not the highest standard. In order to be safe, we must regularly compare our course to that outlined in the Scriptures and continually adjust our lives to it.

Source 4: Circumstances

The fourth area where we can gather evidence of God's will is from circumstances. Not all circumstances are from the Lord, for we are in a war between good and evil. However, we can still sometimes deduce God's will from circumstances. Joseph was sold into slavery by his brothers, but through a chain of circumstances he ended up second in command in Egypt, responsible for storing up food for a famine that God had revealed ahead of time. When the famine happened, Joseph's brothers heard there was food in Egypt and came to purchase some for their families. There they encountered Joseph and were terrified. But he told them, " 'Now do not be grieved or angry with yourselves, because you sold me here, for God sent me before you to preserve life. . . . Now, therefore, it was not you who sent me here, but God' " (Genesis 45:5, 8). Joseph was carried along by circumstances, but God oversaw those circumstances for good. In the same way, circumstances may force us in directions we might not choose ourselves, but through it all God is revealing His will.

The wonderful thing about circumstances is that they do not take much interpretation on our part. One time I interviewed for a job I really wanted, but the company did not extend an offer. That was a clear indication of God's will. If it were God's will for me to have that job, He would have made a way for me to work there. But I certainly cannot go work there if they did not hire me. That is the beauty of circumstances.

The challenge with circumstances is that sometimes the devil will throw roadblocks in our way. If we know for sure that the direction we are going is God's will, and then we are confronted with roadblocks, we need to press forward in God's strength and in faith to overcome those roadblocks.

One time I was praying about our financial situation. We had taken a vacation to the Outer Banks of North Carolina. I was walking down the beach, asking God what we should do next to help us get out of debt and live in an area that was most conducive to spiritual development. A strong impression came into my mind: "You should move to Alaska and homestead." The thought threw me into a quandary. Nothing in the Bible says whether or not one should move to Alaska and homestead. A counselor might think I had lost my mind, but if the impression was from God, I wanted to obey. Nature does not give us any indication. What should I do? How could I verify whether the impression was from God?

I wrestled with this thought for a couple of days. Finally, I thought, *Well, I guess I had better start looking into it.* I went to the library and started doing some research and quickly found that the Homestead Act had been done away with in 1986. At that point it became clear that whatever I thought I heard out there on the beach came from my own imagination. By these circumstances, it was clear that God was not directing us to move to Alaska and homestead.

Source 5: Our Conscience

The fifth area where we can gather evidence about God's will is from our own conscience. Every normal person at some point in their lives possesses an innate sense of right and wrong, even if that person has never read the Bible. People feel good when they do right, and they feel bad when they do wrong. This feeling of right and wrong can be a guide if we are willing to tune in to it. If you have had a child, you may have had the experience of walking around the corner and surprising your child, and they jump, suddenly pretending they are doing some other activity. This shows their conscience at work. They know that whatever they had been doing was wrong.

The conscience can be a guide even for those who do not have access to the Scriptures. Paul wrote,

> When Gentiles who do not have the Law do instinctively the things of the Law, these, not having the Law, are a law to themselves, in that they show the work of the Law written in their hearts, their conscience bearing witness and their thoughts alternately accusing or else defending them (Romans 2:14, 15).

What is important about our conscience is that it serves as the avenue through which all other sources of truth come to us. Therefore, it is vitally important that we pay attention to our conscience. Jesus said,

> "The eye is the lamp of the body; so then if your eye is clear, your whole body will be full of light. But if your eye is bad, your whole body will be full of darkness. If then the light that is in you is darkness, how great is the darkness!" (Matthew 6:22, 23).

If your conscience has gone bad, and you are basing your decisions on your conscience alone and not pulling from all the other sources of truth, your whole life will be filled with darkness. But if we honestly pray to God for a good conscience, and we base our decisions on the full body of evidence rather than just what we feel is right, then our eye is good, so to speak.

The disadvantage with the conscience is that it can go bad. We need to be careful about basing our decisions on intuition alone. Isaiah wrote, "Woe to those who call evil good, and good evil; who substitute darkness for light and light for darkness; who substitute bitter for sweet and sweet for bitter! Woe to those who are wise in their own eyes and clever in their own sight!" (Isaiah 5:20, 21). Our conscience can become warped. In some cases it can be seared as with a hot iron. We have to be careful that in big decisions, moral choices, or otherwise important conclusions, we do not base our determinations on conscience alone, but rather that we gather the evidence from the other sources.

The early reality TV series Rescue 911 was popular when I was a child. It showed real-life emergency situations such as accidents, fires, and crimes, where people called 911 and were rescued. One day the emergency personnel responded to an accident where a woman had crashed into a telephone pole. She was not seriously injured, so at the crash scene the police began interviewing her, asking her what had happened. She replied, "God told me to crash my car into the telephone pole." We may laugh to ourselves, thinking, *How could anybody interpret the will of God like that?* But that poor woman had no adequate filter on her thoughts. When the thought came into her mind, she automatically assumed it was the will of God. That assumption led her to do something that was outside the will of God. One of the Ten Commandments says, "Thou shalt not steal." She was taking something that was not hers—the telephone pole—and destroying it. Another commandment says, "Thou shalt not kill." She was recklessly endangering her own life and the lives of other people. This woman could have discerned even from the Ten Commandments that it was not God's will for her to crash the car into the telephone pole. Her example may be extreme, but we often make the same mistake on lesser levels. Let's keep a filter on our minds and not just assume that any thought that comes into our minds is the will of God.

One time I was working on a test setup to assess a particular product, and we needed some very pure water. Water with even a small amount of particulate would skew the results badly, and therefore we put two large filters on the test system. The filters could take out particulate down to 0.5 microns. If you split a millimeter into two thousand parts, and you took one of those parts, that would be the diameter of the particles that the filters could remove. The first filter would get the vast majority of all the particulate down to 0.5 microns. The second filter would catch the vast majority of the few particles that made it past the first filter. By the time the water came out of that second filter, it was exceedingly clean.

In our lives, we need a filter on our thoughts. The Bible is the very best filter, and the other sources of truth are backup filters. When we think we have heard a message from God, we should test it against the Bible. Does it agree with the Word of God? If it does, then we know for sure that God is speaking to us. If we are uncertain after comparing it with the Bible, we should test out the idea against nature, with godly counselors, and with circumstances. These filters will help us avoid misinterpreting the will of God.

I cringe sometimes when I hear people say, "The Spirit led me . . ." or, "God told me . . ." or, "God laid it on my heart . . ." Maybe He did, but it is altogether too easy to interpret our own desires as the will of God. We should be careful to avoid turning our wishes into spiritual issues. Jeremiah warned, "The heart is deceitful above all things, and desperately wicked" (Jeremiah 17:9, KJV). Far safer is to say, "I wonder if this is God leading?" Then we can take that thought and run it through the filters and see if it stands the test. That will save us from making some serious mistakes.

A man once confided in me that he was having some marriage troubles. He had done some irritating things to his wife, and his wife had said some unkind things to him. His pride had been injured, and he was convinced that there was no hope for them as a couple. This went on for a few months. Finally, he told me, "I have prayed about this situation, and God impressed me that it is better to divorce than to be lost."

I replied, "If what you think you heard disagrees with the Bible, it is not God speaking to you. The Bible says, 'Husbands, love your wives and do not be embittered against them.' It also says, 'Husbands should love their wives as Christ loves the church and gave himself for it to purify her.' 'Husbands, you should love your wives and live with them in an understanding way.' So this is God's will. And this is what God wants from us in marriage."

Now, I know that sometimes marriage can be hard. I already told you that my wife and I ended up in the counselor's office because we could not figure out how to get along. I can understand the hopelessness and the sorrow and sadness one feels in a situation that is less than ideal. But for this man to abandon his wife while she was actively seeking for reconciliation was diametrically opposed to the Word of God.

What I would say to others in similar circumstances is that even if your situation is bad, even if you cannot figure out how to get along, do not lose heart in trying to align your life with God's will. Keep pressing on. God will help you carry out His will, insomuch as it is within your choice to do so. Do not give up just because you feel like it. Certainly, do not spiritualize it and say, "God impressed me to divorce my wife." God says, " 'I hate divorce' " (Malachi 2:16). We need to make sure that our lives are in line with His will.

We have looked at the five major sources for knowing God's will: the Bible, nature, godly counselors, circumstances, and our conscience. However, there is one other important aspect of this evidence-gathering method for knowing God's will, and that is practice. Because understanding God's will is not an exact science, we need to practice it.

A friend of mine was a ham radio operator. In his basement, he had all the equipment set up, and outside he had a sizable antenna. He used the radio to tune in to broadcasts from other ham radio operators, including some communicating with Morse code, which is a series of long and short signals of sound that signify letters of the alphabet. When I heard Morse code coming through my friend's radio equipment, it was unintelligible to me. I could not even begin to make out the various letters, much less the words. But my friend had practiced listening to Morse code for years, and he could decipher in his mind what seemed like gibberish to me. When understanding God's will, it is the same. Paul wrote, "Do not be conformed to this world, but be transformed by the renewing of your mind, so that you may prove what the will of God is, that which is good and acceptable and perfect" (Romans 12:2). Part of being able to discern God's will is that we are transformed by the renewing of our mind. In other words, we practice listening to God's will. When we hear His will, we act on it. The more we do so, the better we get at discerning His will.

The other day a flock of birds landed in my backyard. As they walked across the ground they were looking around the trees, under the leaves, and through the grass. They were on the alert for any little bit of food. We should be that way when it comes to God's will. Every text you read, every walk that you take, every friend with whom you talk, every circumstance in life, and in the quiet thoughts of meditation, search for evidence of God's will. Be always looking for that evidence. Listen in the likely places. Listen in the unlikely places. Listen close. Listen deep. The very best way to understand God's will is to make a habit of gathering the evidence and acting on it.

Discussion Questions:

1. The method suggested in this chapter for knowing God's will can be summarized in one sentence. What is it?

2. What are the five sources listed in this chapter for knowing God's will?

3. Tell what makes the Bible the most authoritative of all of the sources for knowing God's will.

4. Describe how we can identify God's will through "nature."

5. Apply the sources in this chapter to a recent question you have had about God's will. From how many of the sources did you gather the evidence? How do you feel about the quality of your assessment?

6. Draw your own verbal illustration about the value of godly counselors.

7. What pros and cons do you see for each of the sources of evidence regarding God's will?

8. What methods have you used in the past to identify God's will? How are they similar to or different from the method described in this chapter?

9. What would happen if someone does not practice searching these sources for evidence of God's will? What would happen if they practice applying only one or two of the sources?

10. Generate a plan for gathering evidence regarding

God's will. It could be a general plan or, better yet, it could be specifically geared for a situation you are currently facing.

11. The sources listed in this chapter are not necessarily exhaustive. What other sources may exist for knowing God's will? What are the benefits and drawbacks of each?

12. What is your favorite source for truth? Your second favorite? Why?

CHAPTER TEN

The Greatest Mission of All Time

Vapor streamed from the SpaceX Falcon 9 rocket as the last preparations were made for liftoff. Mission control gave the final countdown: "Three, two, one, zero." The rocket engines roared to life, pouring an explosive blast of exhaust across the launch pad and propelling the spacecraft into the sky.

Four minutes into flight, the first stage separated from the second stage. The engine on the second stage fired and sent it accelerating into orbit. Meanwhile, the first stage turned and headed for earth.

The first stage of an orbital rocket had never successfully landed before. Multiple attempts had been made, but each ended in failure. The design team refined this rocket until they thought that the return flight might be successful. Two engine burns slowed the first stage on its descent. The third and final burn lit up the night sky as the spacecraft decelerated toward the landing pad. The employees watched with rising excitement as the landing progressed. The first stage settled down over the landing area as great clouds of fire billowed out below it. Suddenly the fire went out, revealing the first stage standing still and silent amid the clouds of drifting smoke. Thunderous cheers erupted from the employees as they leaped and hugged and celebrated together. History had been made. The mission to safely land the first stage had been accomplished. It was a monumental step toward ushering in a new era of low-cost space flight.[17]

Just as those employees worked so hard on their mission to bring the first stage home, in like manner Jesus gave His disciples instructions that would guide the mission of His church to the end of time. Of critical importance is that that we understand the true meaning of those instructions, for they are the directives that should be the foundation for our lifework.

The key idea I would like us to take away from this chapter is that the Great Commission is a charge to teach people to internalize God's words and act on them. This subject brings us full circle, for the substance of the teaching that Jesus directed His followers to proclaim is none other than the all-important attitude described in Chapter 1. If the Great Commission is heeded, it will lead the hearers into glorious unity with God.

Three Ways to Say the Same Thing

In the Great Commission, Jesus said virtually the same thing in three different ways. He instructed, " 'Go . . . and make disciples of all the nations,' " and then He said it slightly differently: " 'Baptizing them in the name of the Father and the Son and the Holy Spirit.' " And then he described the work a third way: " 'Teaching them to observe all that I have commanded you' " (Matthew 28:19, 20). Suppose I tell my oldest son, "Benjamin, go make the dirty plates shine like new. Scrub them, rinse them, and dry them. Make sure that no spot or stain remains." Have I given him three commands or one? It is one command articulated in three ways.

So, first, we are to make disciples. The Greek word for making

---

17. "ORBCOMM-2 Full Launch Webcast," SpaceX, video presentation, https://www.youtube.com/watch?v=O5bTbVbe4e4

disciples means to teach people to follow God's precepts and instructions. That matches the third phrase, "teaching them to observe all things that I have commanded you." The King James Version translates these two phrases directly, "Go ye therefore, and teach all nations . . . teaching them to observe all things whatsoever I have commanded you." The first and third phrases convey exactly the same thought.

The middle phrase also conveys the thought. Jesus told His disciples to baptize people in the name of the Father, Son, and Holy Spirit. As we studied in Chapter 4, Jesus' name is a state of being, a state of full surrender to Him. Jesus prayed to the Father, " 'Holy Father, keep them in Your name, the name which You have given Me. . . . While I was with them, I was keeping them in Your name which You have given Me" (John 17:11, 12). If we must be kept in God's name, then clearly that name is a place, not a phrase. Baptizing people in the name of the Father, Son, and Holy Spirit does not consist of uttering certain words over them as we immerse them in water. The way we immerse people in the name of the Father, Son, and Holy Spirit is to help them wash away their old sinful life and enter a new way of life, in which they pursue God's will instead. We teach them to forego their natural, corrupt cravings and wholeheartedly respond to God's desires. We teach them to observe all things that He commanded. Therefore we see that all three imperatives in the Great Commission are one and the same.

Baptism Is a Symbol of the Internal Experience

The prerequisite for baptism is that one believes. The Ethiopian eunuch asked Philip if he could be baptized, and Philip replied, "If you believe with all your heart, you may" (Acts 8:37). This belief is much more than a mental assent to the truth. It is a submission to the authority of Christ. The mere immersion of a person in the ceremony of baptism does not mean that that person is saved. The experience of Simon the sorcerer stands as a warning in this regard. Sometime after his baptism, he saw that the Holy Spirit was poured out when the apostles laid their hands on people. He offered money to Peter if he would give him that ability, but Peter replied, " 'May your silver perish with you, because you thought you could obtain the gift of God with money! . . . For I see that you are in the gall of bitterness and in the bondage of iniquity' " (Acts 8:20, 23). Even though Simon had participated in the ceremony of baptism, he did not have the heart experience to which that ceremony pointed. He was on a course to perish because he was still in the bondage of iniquity.

One time Amy and I studied with a couple who were adamant that one could not be saved without undergoing the physical ceremony of baptism. Week after week they returned to the same point, quoting from the book of Mark, saying, " 'He who has believed and has been baptized shall be saved; but he who has disbelieved shall be condemned' " (Mark 16:15, 16). I firmly believe that one cannot be saved without being baptized, but the baptism that saves is a baptism in the name of God—a baptism where we shed the old life and don the new life. Peter framed it well when he said,

Once the longsuffering of God waited in the days of Noah, while the ark was a preparing, wherein few, that is, eight souls were saved by water. The like figure whereunto even baptism doth also now save us (not the putting away of the filth of the flesh, but the answer of a good conscience toward God) (1 Peter 3:20, 21, KJV).

In the physical ceremony of baptism, the dirt is rinsed from the body, but as Peter pointed out, this is just a figure. What saves us is our conscience responding to God in the right way. That response is not a one-time event but an ongoing attitude—the all-important attitude. The attitude that leads to salvation is to wholeheartedly seek to know and do God's will, depending on Him for strength. Physical baptism is the outward symbol of a heart experience. This baptism of the heart is the baptism that saves us.

As Peter alluded to, Noah's experience was also a figure intended to teach something about the true reality. Noah was told to build an ark, and he complied; then God had him enter the ark, along with all of his family. The destruction of the world came, and everybody on earth perished except those sheltered in the ark. Just as Noah entered into the ark, in the same way we must enter into Jesus by receiving His words. Then He abides in us and we abide in Him, just as Noah abided in the ark. Jesus then becomes an ark of safety for us, to shelter us safely through the destruction that is coming on this world. In the end, everybody on earth is going to perish except for those who are in the true ark—those who are in Jesus.

On May 20, 2013, an EF5 tornado roared through Moore, Oklahoma, destroying 1,150 homes and leaving a path of destruction fourteen miles long and up to 1.3 miles wide.[18] One man took a video of the tornado as it approached his in-laws' house. Moments before it hit, he stopped the video and took cover in the home's storm shelter. The tornado swept overhead, and when he emerged a few minutes later, he took a video of the same neighborhood that he had filmed as the tornado approached. Heaps of rubbish now marked the spots where houses had stood moments before. But he and four of his family members were safe because they had taken refuge by entering into that storm shelter.[19] In like manner we must

---

18. "Tornado Devastates Moore, Oklahoma," *CNN*, May 20, 2013, http://www.cnn.com/interactive/2013/05/us/moore-oklahoma-tornado/.

19. Ashton Edwards, "Family Emerges from Storm Shelter to Find Homes Demolished," KFOR, video presentation, http://kfor.com/2013/05/24/video-family-emerges-from-storm-shelter-to-find-homes-demolished/.

take shelter in Jesus by being united with Him through baptism of the heart. He will then protect us from the impending destruction.

The Great Commission's directive to baptize is ultimately a call to help people enter into unity with God. Paul wrote,

> Even as the body is one and yet has many members, and all the members of the body, though they are many, are one body, so also is Christ. For by one Spirit we were all baptized into one body, whether Jews or Greeks, whether slaves or free, and we were all made to drink of one Spirit. . . . Now you are Christ's body, and individually members of it (1 Corinthians 12:12, 13, 27).

When we are baptized with the Spirit, the Spirit becomes part of us, and we thus become part of Christ. Therefore true baptism results in unity with Christ.

Bryan, our middle boy, loves animals. Last spring the cicadas came out in force around our house. Cicadas are slow and easy to catch when they first emerge from their shells. Bryan got up early every morning and hurried outside to gather as many as he could find. He was fascinated by their antics and spent hours watching as the nymphs crawled up the oak trees, fastened their claws into the bark, and prepared to molt. Then they split open their shells, stepped out of them, inflated their wings, and flew away into a completely new way of life. Much like the transformation of those cicadas, the experience of baptism is one where we shed our old way of life and step into a new life. God wants us to help one another in this process. Enabling each other to discover and do God's will is what the Great Commission means when it tells us to baptize people in the name of the Father, Son, and Holy Spirit.

Jesus' Experience with Baptism Is a Model

The baptism Jesus experienced is a model for our baptism.

He was baptized in order to be united with the Father in Spirit. His physical baptism was an outward demonstration of the heart experience He already possessed. This heart experience was one in which He bypassed His own desires and gave Himself up to fulfilling the Father's desires. As soon as Jesus came up out of the water, the Holy Spirit descended on Him in the form of a dove, and a voice came from heaven saying, " 'This is My beloved Son, in whom I am well-pleased' " (Matthew 3:17). His practice of ignoring His own desire to sin and responding wholeheartedly to the Father's desires was what led to the Holy Spirit being poured out on Him and the declaration from the Father that Jesus was His beloved Son.

In a similar way, we are baptized in order to become one with Jesus in the Spirit. The way to become children of God is by having the Holy Spirit, and the way to get the Holy Spirit is to undergo a heart baptism. Paul implored the Romans to consider carefully the true meaning of baptism. He wrote,

> Are we to continue in sin so that grace may increase? May it never be! How shall we who died to sin still live in it? Or do you not know that all of us who have been baptized into Christ Jesus have been baptized into His death? (Romans 6:1–3).

This baptism of the heart brings about a change. We are to relate to our old desires as though we were dead. A dead person does not steal or commit adultery or covet. They just lie in the casket, with no acknowledgement of any such temptation.

One time I played bass with a group at a men's retreat in the Sierra Nevada foothills. We set up the equipment and began to lead the songs, but right in the middle of a song, my bass amplifier began to crackle and pop as though there was a short somewhere in the line. Immediately I checked all of the connections and cords, trying to figure out where the trouble was coming from, and later we opened up the amp and checked the electronics but were unable to locate the source of the problem. Eventually a control switch for one of the two sensors on the bass went dead, and it became apparent that the crackling and popping had come from that broken switch. Subsequently, whenever I played the bass, the signal from that one sensor did not make it through the control switch to the amp. When it comes to our sinful desires, we should be like that faulty control switch. The temptations and desires may be there, but the signal does not get converted into practice, even in thought—there is no response.

However, the other sensor on the bass was also producing a signal, and the control switch for that sensor was good. That signal was passed on to the amp and converted into sound. So we should be when it comes to God's desires. When the Holy Spirit prompts us, the signal from Him should be passed on into our lives and converted into actions.

Paul went on in his letter to the Romans and conveyed this very idea. He wrote,

> Therefore we have been buried with Him through baptism into death, so that as Christ was raised from the dead through the glory of the Father, so we too might walk in newness of life. For if we have become united with Him in the likeness of His death, certainly we shall also be in the likeness of His resurrection. . . . For the death that He died, He died to sin once for all; but the life that He lives, He lives to God. Even so consider yourselves to be dead to sin, but alive to God in Christ Jesus (Romans 6:4, 5, 10, 11).

With respect to sin, we should consider ourselves dead, just like that bass switch was dead. The signal did not pass on through it. But with respect to God we should consider ourselves alive, just like the other bass switch did pass the signal from its sensor on through to the amp. This sort of experience is an ongoing one, in which we daily consider ourselves dead to the former desires and alive to Christ's desires.

In a spiritual sense we should continually be baptized. Paul wrote, "If you are living according to the flesh, you must die; but if by the Spirit you are putting to death the deeds of the body, you will live" (Romans 8:13). Notice that this experience is in the present tense—an ongoing activity. We must daily relate to our old desires as though dead and to God's desires as very much alive. We must be forever searching out His will and acting on it. Therefore baptism is another way of describing the experience of eating and drinking Jesus' teaching, and thereby becoming one with Him.

A Baptism of Repentance

John the Baptist came baptizing people with water, but note carefully that he did not preach a baptism of immersion in water. Mark wrote, "John the Baptist appeared in the wilderness preaching a baptism of repentance for the forgiveness of sins" (Mark 1:4). John used water baptism as a symbol of repentance to help people visualize the invisible heart work. Repentance was the outcome of the experience to which John pointed. He uttered scathing rebukes to the crowds, calling out,

> "You brood of vipers, who warned you to flee from the wrath to come? Therefore bear fruits in keeping with repentance, and do not begin to say to yourselves, 'We have Abraham for our father,' for I say to you that from these stones God is able to raise up children to Abraham. Indeed the axe is already laid at the root of the trees; so every tree that does not bear good fruit is cut down and thrown into the fire" (Luke 3:7-9).

The crowds were convicted by his words, and they questioned him, "Then what shall we do?" His response is revealing. He did not tell them, "Come on down into the river and be baptized." Rather, his directions illuminated the way for people to align themselves with God's will. He said, " 'The man who has two tunics is to share with him who has none; and he who has food is to do likewise.' " And to the tax collectors he said, " 'Collect no more than what you have been ordered to.' " And to the soldiers he said, " 'Do not take money from anyone by force, or accuse anyone falsely, and be content with your wages' " (Luke 3:11–14). Baptizing people in water was a symbol he used to teach about this greater heart work. John's baptism helped people step through their part in the plan of salvation.

The physical ceremony of baptism is still a valuable symbol today. I believe it is biblical and appropriate to baptize people by immersion in water. But let us never forget that it is still a symbol, just as it was in the days of John the Baptist. It points to a deeper heart work—a heart work that is critically important if we hope to enter into life.

Baptism to Prepare the Way for the Lord

The baptism of repentance prepares the way for Jesus to be manifested. John the Baptist testified, " 'I did not recognize Him, but so that He might be manifested to Israel, I came baptizing in water' " (John 1:31). The same is true today. Just as John led the people in a baptism of repentance in order to prepare the way for Jesus, so today it is a baptism of repentance that will prepare the way for the Lord to come again. John the Baptist preached, " 'Repent, for the kingdom of heaven is at hand' " (Matthew 3:2). Jesus took up the same message and preached, " 'Repent, for the kingdom of heaven is at hand' " (Matthew 4:17). On the day of Pentecost, Peter told the people, " 'Repent, and each of you be baptized in the name of Jesus Christ for the forgiveness of your sins; and you will receive the gift of the Holy Spirit' " (Acts 2:38). Repentance—leaving behind the old, sinful life, and beginning the new, Spirit-led life—enables the outpouring of the Holy Spirit.

NASA has two large transport vehicles called crawlers that are used to move spacecraft from the Vehicle Assembly Building to the launch pads. These massive contraptions are more than a hundred feet on a side and weigh about six million pounds. When fully loaded with a launcher platform and rocket, the total weight can exceed seventeen million pounds. These extremely heavy vehicles could not drive out across the bare ground to the launch pads. The crawlers' tracks would sink into the soil, potentially dumping a towering rocket on its side. Therefore a special roadway was prepared on which the crawlers drive. The crawlerway, as it has become known, has a base that is seven feet thick, including layers of fill, crushed stone, and river gravel.[20] The crawlerways have enabled the crawlers to safely move rockets to the launch pads hundreds of times. Just as a special road had to be prepared in order to drive the crawlers, so the way must be prepared for Jesus to return. The way is prepared when we adopt a lifestyle of turning from our former sinful ways and turning to God's desires.

The Baptism of the Holy Spirit

Repentance in and of itself is not the heart of salvation. From the very beginning John the Baptist told the people, " 'I baptize you with water for repentance, but He who is coming after me is mightier than I, and I am not fit to remove His sandals; He will baptize you with the Holy Spirit' " (Matthew 3:11). While repentance is not the heart of salvation, it is the foundation upon which that center is based. The heart of salvation is unity with God. We enter into fellowship with the living, breathing, acting being known as God. Jesus said,

---

20. "Countdown! NASA Launch Vehicles and Facilities," NASA Facts Online, PMS 018-B, Section 3, October 1991, http://www-pao. ksc.nasa.gov/nasafact/count3teaf.htm.

" 'This is eternal life, that they may know You, the only true God, and Jesus Christ whom You have sent' " (John 17:3).

Recently I saw an online video of a young woman opening a Christmas gift from her parents. Her mother handed her a neatly wrapped little package. She tore off the paper and found inside a little box about the size of a set of pens. She lifted the lid, and there lay a key. A look of disbelief came across her face, and she exclaimed, "You're kidding me!" Tears of gratitude began rolling down her face. Her parents suggested she go look in the driveway, and there she found a new car. When the young woman saw the key, she did not exclaim, "Oh, thank you for this beautiful keepsake key. I will treasure it forever as a reminder of this special Christmas." The key was the thing that unlocked a much greater gift. In the same way, baptism in repentance is the key that unlocks a much greater gift—the Holy Spirit.

God with Us

All through the Old Testament God gave promises, living parables, and prophecies revealing something about the heart of salvation, toward which He was working. And when the time came, He revealed Immanuel, "God with us." Jesus is not just with us in the sense of being present nearby, but He becomes an integral part of each person who will follow Him. This is the mystery of God, "Christ in you, the hope of glory . . . . In him dwelleth all the *fulness* of the Godhead bodily, and in him ye are made *full*" (Colossians 1:27; 2:9, 10, ASV, italics supplied).

Paul went on in this passage to explain that this unity with Christ happens when one undergoes a spiritual circumcision. He wrote,

> In Him you were also circumcised with a circumcision made without hands, in the removal of the body of the

flesh by the circumcision of Christ; having been buried with Him in baptism, in which you were also raised up with Him through faith in the working of God, who raised Him from the dead (Colossians 2:11, 12).

Here baptism is compared to circumcision. God gave Abraham the covenant of circumcision, and Abraham consented. He demonstrated that he was willing to part with anything, no matter how personal or painful, if it was God's will. Just as Abraham was physically circumcised, every follower of Christ undergoes a spiritual circumcision. When we determine to keep God's will, that decision is enough for Christ to unite us with Himself, even though we are still loaded down with evil tendencies. With our permission, Christ then cuts away our former sinful ways, and He enables us to live the way He desires.

My wife keeps our family well supplied with fresh home-made bread. She combines the ingredients in her mixer, and at the right time she adds the yeast. Then she turns the mixer on and lets it knead the dough, spreading the yeast thoroughly throughout the batch. She then forms the dough into loaves, and the yeast works in the "midst" of each loaf to cause it to rise and achieve a light and delightful consistency. In a similar sense to the yeast in the loaves, God is in the midst of each of His followers, transforming us from the inside out to be what He desires. He is "God with us."

Exodus records a living parable of what "God with us" really means. Paul talked about this exodus experience in 1 Corinthians 10:1, 2: "I do not want you to be unaware, brethren, that our fathers were all under the cloud and all passed through the sea; and all were baptized into Moses in the cloud and in the sea." Here Paul was referring to the cloud that shaded the Israelites during the day and the fiery pillar that gave them light by night. Isaiah also talked about that cloud, and he tied it together with the tabernacle. He said,

The LORD will create upon every dwelling place of mount Zion, and upon her assemblies, a cloud and smoke by day, and the shining of a flaming fire by night. For upon all the glory shall be a defence. And there shall be a tabernacle for a shadow in the daytime from the heat, and for a place of refuge, and for a covert from storm and from rain (Isaiah 4:5, 6, KJV).

Note that the tabernacle was a shadow in the daytime from the heat, just as the pillar of cloud shaded the Israelites. The cloud itself was a tabernacle. It was impractical for the Israelites to build a tabernacle that would house well over a million people (an estimate of how many came out of Egypt). Instead, God instructed them in how to build a tabernacle in small form, and then He caused His physical presence to emanate from that tabernacle in the form of the pillar of cloud that covered the whole congregation. The cloud was an extension of the sanctuary. Therefore the Israelites symbolically dwelled in the sanctuary. In like manner, Jesus is the sanctuary for His people.

When our oldest boy was two years old, I took him backpacking in the Shining Rock Wilderness in North Carolina. We set up our camp for the weekend in a sturdy group of pine trees. The next day we hiked along the ridge, enjoying the spectacular views, and eventually started returning toward camp. We were nearly back when a storm caught us. Sheets of rain descended and quickly drenched our clothes. I grabbed Benjamin and hurriedly carried him the last few hundred yards. We stepped into the pine trees and dived into the sturdy four-season tent. The rain beat on the outside, and the wind shook the tent flaps, but we were sheltered inside. There we dried off, put on clean clothes, and waited until the rain passed. That tent was a welcome reprieve from the elements. We entered it, and it sheltered us. In a similar way, Jesus is a shelter, a sanctuary, for those who are baptized into Him.

Isaiah prophesied, " 'It is the LORD of Hosts whom you should regard as holy. And He shall be your fear, and He shall be your dread. Then He shall become a sanctuary' " (8:13, 14). When He is our fear and our dread, and we regard Him as holy—when we have the right attitude toward Him—then He becomes a sanctuary for us. And it goes on, " 'But to both the houses of Israel, a stone to strike and a rock to stumble over, and a snare and a trap for the inhabitants of Jerusalem. Many will stumble over them. Then they will fall and be broken. They will even be snared and caught' " (verses 14, 15). Finally it says, " 'Bind up the testimony, seal the law among my disciples' " (verse 16). So who are the ones who were called His disciples? His disciples are those who have the law bound up in their hearts and the testimony sealed within them. Those who fear the Lord and regard Him as holy—these are his disciples. And for His disciples, He becomes a sanctuary.

Not only is Jesus a temple for those who believe in Him, but believers are a temple for Him. Here we find another aspect of what it means for Him to be "Immanuel . . . God with us." Isaiah prophesied,

> Thus says the LORD, "Heaven is My throne and the earth is My footstool. Where then is a house you could build for Me? And where is a place that I may rest? For My hand made all these things, thus all these things came into being," declares the LORD. "But to this one I will look, to him who is humble and contrite of spirit, and who trembles at My word" (Isaiah 66:1, 2).

Those who are humble, contrite, and who tremble at His word become a dwelling place for God. These characteristics of humility, contrition, and holy fear are another way of describing the all-important attitude required for entering into unity with God.

The corporation where I work just acquired a startup

company with an attractive new product. Out of curiosity, I zoomed in on the company's location with Google Street View and was amazed to see a house in a neighborhood. Apparently the startup was located in somebody's garage. As I write this, my corporation has 85,000 employees and annual revenue of more than $28 billion. We took the technology from that tiny startup and infused it with our engineering resources, distribution channels, and reputation. Thus it transformed their product from little more than a nice idea into a revolutionary technology. In a similar way, those who internalize God's words become united with Him. He dwells within them and infuses them with His character, power, and love. This unity with God is the heart of salvation to which the baptism of repentance leads.

When Moses was tending sheep in the desert, he was surprised to see a bush that was blazing with fire but was not consumed. He moved closer to inspect the marvelous sight. God then called to him from the midst of the bush and said, "Moses . . . do not come near here; remove your sandals from your feet, for the place on which you are standing is holy ground" (Exodus 3:4, 5). God went on to declare that He was the God of Abraham, Isaac, and Jacob. To these three individuals God had given the promises regarding a coming seed. To Abraham He described the seed (singular) as the countless stars of the heaven. To him He also described that seed as the innumerable sand of the seashore. To Jacob He depicted that one seed as a ladder that connected earth and heaven. To Moses He portrayed the same mystery, this time as a burning bush.

God declared to Moses, " 'Israel is My son, My firstborn' " (Exodus 4:22). The nation of Israel was referred to as singular, even though the population of it was many hundreds of thousands. The one firstborn was made up of many individuals, just as God had promised that the one seed would be like the sand of the sea and like the stars of the heavens.

Note two things: first, Jesus is the only Son of the Father (John 3:16). Second, Jesus is the firstborn among many brethren (Romans 8:29), even though He was born more than a thousand years after God declared that Israel was His firstborn. At first these statements may seem mutually exclusive, but it was in anticipation of the unity between Christ and His people that God could call the nation of Israel His son. And it was also in anticipation of this unity that God could call the nation of Israel not just His son but His firstborn.

This unity was what God was trying to describe to Moses through the symbol of the burning bush. This one bush had many branches, and the glory of God was blazing from its midst. Jesus likened Himself to a vine and His followers to the branches. His life flowing through us is what gives us life. Jesus is the bush, we are the branches, and the glory of the Father blazes forth within us through the Holy Spirit.

Moses was not allowed to approach the bush. He could only view its glory from a distance. In like manner, God showed Moses many great symbols of the unity that God's followers would have with Him, but the time had not yet come. Moses could only look down into the distant future and view the glory of God shining from within His people. In Moses' day, the Holy Spirit was operating as a separate entity from people, not as one with the followers of God. Not until after Jesus was glorified was the Holy Spirit given (John 7:39; 14:17). On the day of Pentecost, when the Holy Spirit first assumed His new role, tongues of fire appeared, separated, and came to rest upon each person present. The glory of God was at last shining forth from the midst of the branches of Jesus.

This message of unity with God is of critical importance. The apostle John warned,

> By this you know the Spirit of God: every spirit that confesses that Jesus Christ has come in the flesh is from

God; and every spirit that does not confess Jesus is not from God; this is the spirit of the antichrist, of which you have heard that it is coming, and now it is already in the world. You are from God, little children, and have over-come them; because greater is He who is *in you* than he who is in the world (1 John 4:2–4, italics supplied).

The spirit of the antichrist is the one that denies Jesus has come in the flesh. What does it mean for Him to "come in the flesh"? Verse 4 clarifies that Jesus has come in *our* flesh, and the spirit of the antichrist is the one who denies that. Any person who rejects the need for Christ to come into his or her life in the form of Jesus' teachings is embracing the spirit of the antichrist. In contrast, we should confess Christ; in other words, we should acknowledge and embrace the necessity of Christ dwelling in us in the form of His words. We should embrace the all-important attitude that leads to a life-giving relationship with God—to wholeheartedly seek out and act on the teachings of Christ, depending on Him for strength.

The Great Commission is a charge to teach people to in-ternalize God's words and act on them. Not only are we to embrace unity with God for ourselves, we are to help others enter that unity as well. To make disciples of all nations, in-structing them to observe the all-important attitude from which flows all of the wonders of unity with God, is our com-mission. To help them shed the old, sinful way of life and en-ter a new life—one that is fully surrendered to God—is our commission. To teach them to respond as dead to their sin-ful desires, and respond in a lively way to God's desires—that too is our commission. We are to facilitate them entering the name of the Father, Son, and Holy Spirit—entering a state of being where they are fully surrendered to His will. Then His glory will blaze forth from within each of them in the form of the Holy Spirit. This outcome is the purpose of the Great Commission.

Authority from on High

God has not left us alone to carry this gospel of the kingdom to all nations. When He gave the Great Commission to the disciples, He sandwiched it between two messages of encouragement. He told them, " 'All authority has been given to Me in heaven and on earth. . . . Lo, I am with you always, even to the end of the age' " (Matthew 28:18, 20). Jesus wanted to assure His disciples that He could help them carry out what He was asking them to do, and He wanted them to know that they would never be alone in their efforts to fulfill the task He gave them.

In the Great Commission Jesus clearly stated His will. That means that if we pray in His name—in a state of surrender to Him and in accordance with His will—then with mighty power He will help us carry out the commission. He has promised, " 'I will never desert you, nor will I ever forsake you' " (Hebrews 13:5). And He has said, " 'Do not fear, for I am with you; do not anxiously look about you, for I am your God. I will strengthen you, surely I will help you, surely I will uphold you with My righteous right hand' " (Isaiah 41:10). The mission Jesus gave us is to unite people with Him—this is our highest duty. We should focus our efforts on carrying out this work.

Someone once told me it was possible to start a fire with a magnifying glass. One day I decided to test out the theory. A stack of corrugated cardboard worked well for tinder. A few adjustments to the position and tilt of the magnifying glass brought the light into a brilliant pinpoint on the cardboard's surface. A moment later the cardboard blackened and a wisp of smoke rose into the air. It began to glow red and smolder down through the layers. A minute or so later, a yellow flame leaped from the stack, and soon the whole pile was engulfed in fire. Just as the focused beam of light can ignite a fire, in like manner we should carefully adjust our efforts so that they are focused on carrying out the mission of uniting people to God.

Unity with God hinges on adopting the all-important attitude. That unity with Him results in a host of additional blessings, including unity with fellow believers, guaranteed answers to prayer, the restoration of the true worship of God, the preaching of the kingdom to the whole world, and the preparation of the way for Jesus to come. Therefore it is of utmost importance that we teach people the extreme gravity of this attitude. We have a mission to fulfill. Will you join me? Let's press forward in the strength of God to carry this message to our homes, to our workplaces, to our churches, to our communities, and to the ends of the earth.

Discussion Questions:

1. What is the heart of salvation?

2. What is "the mystery of God"?

3. What is the relationship between the Great Commission and the all-important attitude?

4. In your own words, paraphrase how the three commands contained in the Great Commission are in actuality only different ways of saying the same thing.

5. If someone asked you the meaning of baptism, what would you tell them?

6. A baptism of repentance prepares the way for the Lord. Sketch a verbal illustration of this concept.

7. Can one be saved without being baptized? Explain.

8. What is the difference between the baptism of repentance and the baptism of the Holy Spirit? How are they related?

9. Christ said that all authority in heaven and on earth has been given to Him. How can we better tap into

that power for carrying out the Great Commission?

10. The overarching themes of this book all tie together in the Great Commission. Pick two or three chapters from this book and identify the main theme from each one. Describe how they are related to the Great Commission.

11. In carrying out the Great Commission, what is the role of human effort versus reliance upon God's power?

12. Assess your current efforts to carry out the Great Commission. Based on the information you learned from this chapter, what is going well? What might you do differently going forward?